Queenie's

A Schoolgirl's Life

1914 – 1915

by

'Queenie' Elsie Llewella Jones

Edited by

Margaret Cook

and

Helen Pullar

Agneau Press

First published July 2005 by Agneau Press
20 Essex Court, Bellbird Park Qld 4300
Australia

Reprinted October 2005

Printed in Australia by The Printing Office

ISBN 0 9580489 2 4

Cover illustration by Chris Platt

Queenie

The diary

Queenie Jones commenced writing a diary on 1 January 1914. On that day she notes *Got a bet on, of an icecream, to keep diary full, with C. Robinson, so keep it up.*

Her diary entry on 31 December records *Am looking forward to two ice-creams.* So she won the bet and was to be a prolific diarist for much of her life.

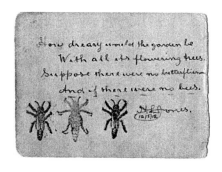

*How dreary would the garden be
With all its flowers and trees,
Suppose there were no butterflies
And if there were no bees.*

H.L Jones   12/5/12

Penned in Queenie's autograph book by her father Harry Jones

Many of the photos reproduced in this book were of poor quality and therefore are not very clear.

The editors felt, however, that they would give the reader a real sense of the period and lifestyle described in the pages of the diary.

Previous page: Queenie Jones at IGGS in 1915 from her own photograph album.

Contents

Queenie's Home

This photo of 'Oakleigh' was taken in 1933 and is labelled 'Beekeepers' 'Field Day'

Queenie's School

Ipswich Girls' Grammar School

Foreword

For someone with a great interest in social history and a special love for the history of Ipswich Girls' Grammar School (IGGS), I was delighted when my daughter Margaret Cook, the IGGS Archivist, passed on to me the news that she had been contacted by Mrs Claire Wilson whose mother Queenie Jones had attended IGGS in 1914 and 1915.

During those years Queenie had kept a diary in which she had recorded the daily events of her life, both at school and at her home in Redbank Plains.

Claire was painstakingly transcribing the 1915 diary which, though written in pencil and in a very small hand, was still reasonably intact. She wondered if we would be interested in having a copy in the archives and perhaps the 1914 one as well if she were to persevere with her transcription.

"Would we be interested?" Margaret and I were 'blown away'! We met with Claire who not only gave us the manuscript but provided electronic copy as well, together with some wonderful memorabilia from Queenie's schooldays.

Our delight grew as we read the pages of the diaries and within a very short space of time we both felt that this was something worth sharing. "Would you allow us to publish them?", we asked Claire. Now it was Claire's turn to be 'blown away' as she had not anticipated such an enthusiastic response.

I floated the idea with the IGGS Old Girls Association Committee and their reaction was so encouraging that Margaret and I decided that this was an enterprise which simply had to come to fruition.

Not surprisingly, the project grew 'like Topsy' as we became increasingly fascinated by the history of Queenie's family, her references to IGGS, her accounts of life at 'Oakleigh' and the insight her writings gave to that very important period of history.

1

Margaret undertook the research which has placed the diaries in context. Gaining an understanding of Queenie's family and her life at 'Oakleigh' Redbank Plains was greatly helped by Claire Wilson and her family. Through several chats and visits she generously responded to endless questions and allowed us to share her family memories and memorabilia. A treasure trove of family albums, Queenie's autograph books, bee-keeping manuals and a family history[1] were shared with us.

A visit to Redbank Plains School and the Yarrow Centre provided further information, supplemented by research material provided by Ipswich City Council Library. Through these sources and family anecdotes we have been able to piece together the story of Queenie's home life, and through our IGGS archival material we built up an understanding and embellishment of her boarding life at IGGS.

Gradually the project took on a momentum of its own. We were greatly helped by local Ipswich writer Pamela Lamb whose publishing company Agneau Press printed the finished product. Pam's son Chris Platt designed the cover and both willingly gave advice.

While Margaret and I researched, collated, wrote and desktop published the contextual information, my husband Ian set out the diaries as closely as possible to the original.

The final product is one which we hope will give pleasure to many readers, whether or not they have connections with IGGS or the Ipswich area.

We would like to thank the IGGSOGA for backing the project and all those who have helped along the way.

We specially thank Queenie whose dedication and tenacity (or love of icecream) resulted in this amazing little insight into life early last century.

Helen Pullar

From the archivist

Presented with the exciting project of publishing Queenie's diaries, it seemed essential to us that they be placed in their context of life at Ipswich Girls' Grammar School as well as 'Oakleigh', Redbank Plains.

Working with the diaries, I extracted details such as names of the teachers and students and the various activities of the school.

IGGS is extremely fortunate to hold a rich archive collection, compiled over the years from school records and donations from the community. It was this collection that made contextualising the diaries possible.

Reference to the school magazines from the 1910s helped add considerable detail to the events described in Queenie's diaries. The school magazines, for example, provide colourful accounts of the school bazaars, dances and the war effort noted by Queenie.

The school photograph collection held some photographs of staff and students from Queenie's day as well as photographs of the buildings, tennis courts and grounds, many of which are reproduced in this book.

IGGS is extremely fortunate to hold the original roll books, two large leather bound volumes which record many details of the girls who have attended the school from its 1892 foundation year to 1971. From these roll books I was able to glean more details about Queenie and her friends.

Thalia Kennedy's book *The First One Hundred Years*[2] was particularly helpful in providing information on the staff and early school prospectuses were also a great source of information and photos.

From these archival sources and personal knowledge, the editors have been able to draw a picture of life at IGGS as Queenie recounts in her diaries.

Margaret Cook

Page 153: 1915 diary

"No visitors for a marvellous wonder!"

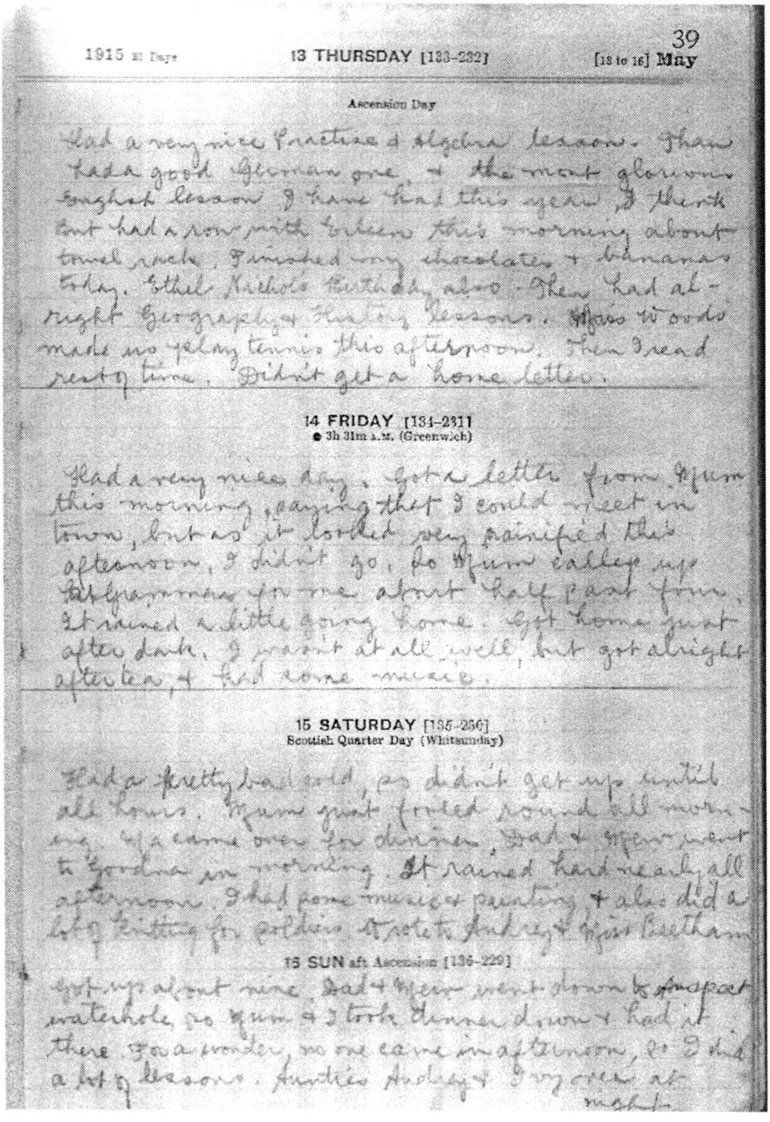

1915 [illegible] Days | 13 THURSDAY [133-232] | 39 [13 to 16] May

Ascension Day

Had a very nice Practice & algebra lesson. Then had a good German one, & the most glorious English lesson I have had this year, I think. But had a row with Eileen this morning about towel rack. Finished my chocolates & bananas today. Ethel Nichols Birthday also. Then had alright Geography & History lessons. Miss Woods made us play tennis this afternoon. Then I read rest of time. Didn't get a home letter.

14 FRIDAY [134-231]
3h 31m A.M. (Greenwich)

Had a very nice day. Got a letter from Mum this morning, saying that I could meet in town, but as it looked very rainified this afternoon, I didn't go, so Mum called up at Grammar for me about half past four. It rained a little going home. Got home just after dark. I wasn't at all well, but got alright after tea, & had some music.

15 SATURDAY [135-230]
Scottish Quarter Day (Whitsunday)

Had a pretty bad cold, so didn't get up until all hours. Mum just fooled round all morning. [illegible] came over for dinner. Dad & Merv went to Goodna in morning. It rained hard nearly all afternoon. I had some music & painting & also did a lot of knitting for soldiers. Wrote to Audrey & Miss Beetham.

16 SUN aft Ascension [136-229]

Got up about nine. Dad & Merv went down to inspect waterhole, so Mum & I took dinner down & had it there. For a wonder, no one came in afternoon, so I did a lot of lessons. Auntie, Audrey & [illegible] over at night.

Queenie Jones

The author of these diaries was 'Queenie' Elsie Llewella Jones who was a weekly boarder at Ipswich Girls' Grammar School in 1914 and 1915. Born on 20 April 1899, she was the eldest child of Harry and Elsie Jones, early settlers at Redbank Plains.

Queenie's grandfather, Lewis Jones, farmer and grazier, was born in Brecon, South Wales, in 1824. Like many Welshmen he was involved in the coal and iron trades. He married in 1851, migrating to Australia in 1862 with his wife, Martha, and his sons Daniel and James. Three years later they settled at Redbank Plains where a third son, Henry Lewis, was born. Lewis initially worked for the Redbank Coal Company and then for the railways on the main railway line. After settling at Redbank Plains he successfully grew cotton on his 300 acre property. The cotton industry at the time was experiencing a boom because of closed access to the American markets during the Civil War. When the industry later proved to be not viable, Lewis turned to grazing and horse breeding.

An adherent of the Congregational Church, Lewis Jones was *esteemed in the district as one of its earliest and most energetic settlers and an upright resident.*[3] The family was very well known in the district.

In 1887 the eldest son Daniel built an imposing residence, 'Oakleigh' at Redbank Plains, complete with orchard and an avenue of mango trees leading to the front steps. Interested in cotton growing and known as 'The Cotton King', Daniel had aspirations to enter Parliament but these hopes failed to eventuate.[4]

His younger brother Henry ('Harry') Lewis purchased 'Oakleigh' and in 1898 moved in with his new bride, Charlotte Elsie (known as 'Elsie'), daughter of James and Louisa Campbell. The Campbells were also Redbank Plains settlers and they feature in Queenie's accounts of daily life at 'Oakleigh'.

This early photo of 'Oakleigh' is pre-1920 as that was when the detached kitchen seen on the right burned down.

Harry and Elsie produced four children, Elsie Llewella (known as 'Queenie'), Henry Mervyn (known as 'Merv', born on 7 September 1900), Audrey Myrtle (born on 13 March 1902) and Valma Rae (born on 5 August 1918).

Since school Harry Jones had been interested in bee keeping and had established an apiary at the family home 'Pentwyn' at Redbank Plains.

He later established the 'Mel Bonum' (good honey) Apiaries at 'Oakleigh' which became the biggest Queen Bee-breeding establishment in the Southern Hemisphere.

The apiary at 'Pentwyn'

Harry examining his bees

He imported pure Italian bees and established a world-wide reputation. He produced a magazine and bee-keeping catalogues which became institutions in the industry. He was President of the Queensland Bee-keepers Association from 1904 to 1920 and established a factory in Goodna to build equipment for the industry and a sawmill to provide timber for bee boxes.

Harry called his infant daughter, Elsie, his 'little Queen Bee' and she became known as Queenie, the name she answered to all of her life.

Harry was an enthusiast in all his activities and had a reputation for efficiency and straight dealing. These activities ranged from horseback bush excursions to involvement in local affairs and politics. He was the first Chairman of the Moreton Shire Council in the year 1917, and was again elected in 1921 and remained Chairman until 1930.

Queenie's mother, Elsie, was a gracious hostess and excellent cook, as well as being involved in local affairs. She established the first branch of the Country Women's Association at Redbank Plains, serving as its foundation President. After the family moved to Goodna she established a branch in that area too. She was a tireless worker for charities as can be seen in the pages of the diaries.

Queenie's Aunt May Campbell, Queenie and Queenie's mother, Elsie Jones (née Campbell)

A much-loved family photo of Merv and Queenie

For Merv, growing up at 'Oakleigh' was an adventure of bees, bush, horses and sport. At Ipswich Grammar School (IGS) he excelled at tennis and later became Open Singles Champion of Ipswich.

After his father's death in 1932, Merv took over the Apiary and continued for the next twenty-three years. When he married Edith Benn in 1935, 'Oakleigh' became their home and they raised four sons and one daughter. 'Oakleigh' was sold in 1957.

Merv with Dot Mansfield who won the Mixed Doubles Championship with him.

9

Despite being blind from the age of three, the second daughter, Audrey, became a gifted pianist who obtained her letters for Music. In 1933 she won the Open Pianoforte Solo section of the Queensland Eisteddfod at Ipswich. Audrey was a foundation member of the Queensland Literary, Musical & Self-Aid Society for the Blind. She had a lovely soprano voice and was part of a blind Concert Party that toured the state fund-raising for the Society.

Audrey was a highly skilled knitter and bought herself a piano with the proceeds of her knitting. Throughout her life she loved to listen to cricket and football on the radio. In her later years she gave many hours as a volunteer pianist for Music Therapy in a retirement village.

Welcomed into the Jones family as a 'late baby', Valma had a very happy childhood at 'Oakleigh'. In 1933 she boarded briefly at IGGS, along with her cousin Olive Campbell. Later she trained at Ipswich Hospital, eventually becoming a Triple-Certificated Nursing Sister.

Valma married Norm Jackson (a 'Rat of Tobruk') in 1946 and they raised two daughters and two sons at Chelmer. Widowed in 1998, Val now lives at Currumbin Waters.

Audrey pumping up water for Valma

Music, tennis, horses, mangoes, the bush and the bees were all magnets that attracted people to 'Oakleigh' from afar. Queenie adored her life at 'Oakleigh'.

The orchard-lined drive up to 'Oakleigh'

Queenie recalled in the family history

My childhood memories are of a large two-storey home and a large orchard . . . innumerable billy-boiling picnics, hikes or horse rides to White Rock area and Spring Mountain; camping overnight and tramping around the bush at night with Merv looking for possums.

This was before the day of the motor car, but we always had company. Professors, doctors and scientists used to stay weekends and tap over the bushland for fossil fish .. . . Sir Arthur and Lady Conan Doyle's visit was a highlight.

Politicians used to dine with us before their meetings at the local school where Dad presided. My first car drive was in the car of the Queensland Premier, the Hon. Digby Denham.

*As we children grew up, Dad had a tennis court
built. Every Sunday afternoon friends came from
Ipswich or Brisbane to play and have afternoon
tea under the mango trees. We often had up to
thirty people.
Music usually followed and sometimes dancing
on the big open verandah.⁵*

Tennis at 'Oakleigh'

Queenie loved the horseback adventures with her father, brother
and friends, sometimes involving overnight campouts at places such
as Spring Mountain. She delighted in the company of the young
Queensland University geologists who frequented 'Oakleigh' after
fossils were discovered on the Jones' property. After the advent of
the motor-car there were also many happy excursions to the South
Coast.

After her two years at IGGS, Queenie attended the Ipswich Tech-
nical College, where she excelled in commercial subjects. She then
became her father's Secretary/Book-keeper, sometimes working in
the office upstairs at 'Oakleigh' until late at night.

All that was good about 'Oakleigh' : the company, the horses, the mangoes

Along with her mother and Campbell aunts, Queenie contributed enthusiastically to the WWI war effort at Redbank Plains, mainly through involvement in local fund-raising plays and concerts. She and her mother would bake for days before these events.

A fundraising play at Greenwood Village Hall.
Queenie third from left in back row with her
mother centre of front row

Queenie would spend hours helping Audrey memorise new piano pieces, or reading books to her and her blind friends. Twice she was chaperone for a group of blind musicians on their fund-raising tours of western and northern Queensland.

In 1930 Queenie married Englishman Edwin ('Ted') Evans in St. Paul's Church, Ipswich. The newly-weds moved into a house built by her father at Goodna beside the factory used by his Bee-goods manufacturing company, H.L. Jones & Sons. Ted took over management of the factory with Queenie once again in the role of office worker at home.

Queenie and Ted produced three daughters – Shirley (1932), Claire (1933) and Kaye (1941). Ted later became involved with the promotion of the honey industry. Queenie, with her office skills and her 'way with words' was his able assistant until his death in 1954.

Queenie on her wedding day

Queenie's father, Harry, died in 1932, eight days after the birth of his first grandchild. After her mother Elsie's death in 1951, Audrey lived with Queenie, first at Goodna, then in Brisbane until Queenie's death in 1973. Together they had become much loved and valued baby-sitters for Queenie's three granddaughters and seven grandsons.

The pages of the diaries refer constantly to family members at 'Oakleigh', as well as numerous visitors who came for mangoes, honey or the social activities which were such a feature of the Jones' life.

14

Honey was used in all Queenie's cooking.
Here daughter Claire joins her mother in a
promotional activity.

The diaries also refer to a long-term house-guest Mr Chappell who was a wealthy Englishman who had come out to Australia to propose marriage (albeit unsuccessfully) to Miss Frances Wilde, the first Matron of St. Andrew's Hospital at Ipswich. There are also references throughout to Miss Shepherd who was a teacher at Audrey's school.

There are many references to 'The Farm' at Redbank Plains. Grandpa James Campbell worked out west but Grandmother Louisa ('Ma') lived at 'The Farm' with Aunts Rosie, Audrey and Ivy and Cousins Ivors, Audrey and Keith Barns, the orphaned children of May (née Campbell). Other family members came and went from time to time. The constant visiting from one property to the other is well documented.[6]

Page 70:   1914 Diary

"My first day at Grammar."

Purification of V. Mary. Candlemas.
Scottish Quarter Day

My first day at Grammar School. Came
to school with Phyllis in the morning.
Enjoyed a few lessons but did not
like others. Missed my music lesson
but practised in the afternoon after
school. I am now going to bed. It
is nearly nine o'clock. Like school
fairly well. Ordered my books.

3 TUESDAY [34-331]
) 10h 33m A.M. (Greenwich)

Bright and better today. I had two
practices of music. Was with Phil
nearly all day. Am now going
to bed. It is about nine o'clock.
Liked my lessons better today. Had
and had home lessons than last
night. My books used.

4 WEDNESDAY [35-330]

Liked school still better today. Had
my music lesson this afternoon &
practised for an hour this morning.
Wrote a letter to a woman this
morning. Also and posted it.
Had a game of piano this evening.
Am now going to bed. But I find
every now gas is on the whole up.

10 mls later. I don't enjoy
myself this 1st week.

Queenie's School in 1914

The diary is delightfully frank. As you read the following pages you may well be struck by similarities with your own school days and certainly those of present school students. Queenie's diaries are peppered with comments on horrendous exams; fear or delight about examination marks; assessments of teachers' moods and her eager anticipation of social activities and school holidays.

The pages of Queenie's 1914 diary which relate to Ipswich Girls' Grammar cover the school year from 2 February 1914 until the last school day that year, 9 December. Queenie was one of 56 boarders who attended the school in 1914. As she lived as far away as Redbank Plains she was a weekly boarder, travelling by sulky or train from Goodna each Friday and Monday of term. Contact during the week with her family came more days than not by letter, rather than the telephone or email contact that today's boarders enjoy. These letters were eagerly anticipated. If her family were in town they would visit and sometimes bring food.

17

It is hard for us to imagine a life-style in which a girl from Redbank Plains, today an outer Ipswich suburb, would need to be a weekly boarder. There were, of course no local high schools, the first of these in Queensland being established in 1912.

By 1914, Ipswich Girls' Grammar School (or the GGSI – Girls' Grammar School Ipswich as it was more familiarly known) had been established for 22 years. It was still a relatively small school and Queenie was only the 629th student to enrol.[7]

By 1914 the school comprised the original building, designed by architect George Brockwell Gill, with its 1901 additional northern wing with the distinctive turret, the Lodge at the Queen Victoria Parade entrance, the play-shed and a gymnasium. In 1910 a much-welcomed new wing was added which greatly added to the boarders' comfort with a new dining room and additional dormitories.

In 1911 a new classroom, an art studio, music rooms and a new tennis court were acquired, though the music room was later re-moved to the site of the old stables as it was deemed to be too noisy in its former situation.

Undoubtedly, it is this noise which is referred to in the June 1914 Magazine.

A view from the northern face of the school showing the 1910 extensions

The Art Studio

Many and varied are the uses the Studio is put to now-a-days, and if it is true that walls have ears, then, indeed these same walls must suffer stony martyrdom from the excruciating sounds that proceed from the occupants of this room; indeed, I am inclined to think that it must be true that walls have ears for I have noticed long cracks in them, caused, no doubt, by the ear-splitting sounds from hastily-tuned violins etc.

The school was growing, not only in bricks and mortar but also in enrolments and The Editorial of the same Magazine states

This year there is a distinctly new element in the School. A large proportion of the girls left last year, and their places have all been filled by new students. It is for these students to enter into the spirit of the life here. They have a large responsibility.

This classroom was set up at one end of the Assembly Hall. The somewhat alarming chairs were 'Dr Roth's special chairs for girls' which were adjustable and no doubt ensured that the young ladies maintained the correct posture while sitting at their desks.

Poor Queenie! It is not difficult to ascertain from the diary entries that quite often IGGS came a poor second to her wonderful life at 'Oakleigh'! Nevertheless, she did seem for the most part to enjoy her life at 'the GGSI' as she called it.

Queenie attended IGGS for two years and was able to sit for her Junior at the end of this time. While some of Queenie's friends were at IGGS for five years or more (see chapter entitled *Queenie's Friends)*, it was more normal to leave school at the end of the Junior year as very few girls enjoyed the luxury of remaining at school to complete further study to matriculation standard.

Junior standard was not necessarily reached in just two years and it is apparent that some students did not sit for the Public Examinations at all. Those who did sit for the Junior were Vth Formers, while the VIth Formers undertook the Senior Examination, presumably after an additional two years of study beyond Junior.

If we look at the Form Notes in the June 1914 Magazine we will see that there are Third Form, Lower IV Form (sic), Fourth Form, Fifth Form and Sixth Form notes. In the December 1915 edition, there are Lower Fourth, IV Form, Lower Fifth and Sixth Form notes. On 27 October Queenie records *Miss Cribb as much as told me I was going into V form* and then on 20 November she writes *My last day in Upper Fourth.*

In the December 1917 Magazine, the V Formers write *We find ourselves ebbing in proportion as the Junior approaches.* Exactly how students were allotted their designated forms, one imagines, was a factor of their academic standard.

Quite a deal was made of the examination students it seems. In *The First One Hundred Years* Cecilia Holland (née Brown) who attended IGGS in 1913 and 1914 writes

> *When the students for the Junior exam were going off in the horse-drawn charabanc we would go and farewell them and wish them luck.*[8]

Queenie would have slept in a dormitory similar to this

It would seem that some aspects of boarders' lives have not changed much throughout the history of Ipswich Girls' Grammar. Queenie's diary talks of short sheeting beds and chatting way after lights out. Like all boarders, she and her friends are ever on the lookout for the teachers on boarding duty as they stretch the lights-out rules. Many times she is racing the clock *Miss Hill has told us to put out our light so must hurry up*, on 27 July. On 11 November she writes *writing this in dark so must shut up*.

Queenie's descriptions of her teachers' moods leave little to the imagination. On 29 October *Miss Lilley was in a most glorious humour for English*. This was not the case on 20 July when *Miss Lilley in a good bit of a temper*.

Comments on Miss White, the Headmistress, were not off limits. On 25 June *Miss White in an awful rats. Said we were all luna-tics except about six – hope I'm one of these*. Another time, 25 March, she wrote, *this afternoon was summoned before the court of Lilley (Miss Lilley's room) where I received such a lecture on my most fearful writing*.

Her diary is also punctuated with the usual student stress about study. On 25 March she writes *am at my wit's ends I have so much to do for tomorrow*. On 27 July Queenie says *new time-table today – pretty hard one, but managed to scrape through somehow*. On 22 March Queenie is *nearly standing on my head so much in a whirlwind with lessons for tomorrow. Something cruel!*

Not all days were bad, however. Queenie records that 26 June was a *Bonser day*. Perhaps that was because it was a short day, as they left before 3 o'clock. On Wednesday 11 November she

> *had a very nice day. Had a pretty fair music lesson. Then enjoyed algebra very much. Had a lovely English exam – so I thought, but alas! For my thoughts, – they were absolutely all wrong. Had an alright History lesson – better than usual.*

Her first day in Fifth Form, 23 November was a particularly good day. *Had a most angelic, beautiful, sweet dream of an English lesson today. Also had a pretty extra-special nice German lesson.*

A highlight of the year was receiving two prizes at Speech Night. On 9 December she writes *found to the surprise of my life that I had got two prizes – Geography & Junior Book-keeping.*

It is interesting to note in this Prize List as well as the Academic Prizes, there were awards for Good Conduct, Homework, Gymnastics, Tennis, Music prizes, Poetry, Painting and Drawing, Needlework and Fancy Work.

The June 1915 Magazine tells us

> *On Wednesday December 9th, 1914, we packed up all our books with light and joyous hearts, and proceeded to make our preparations for the important ceremony of the annual prize-giving.*

> *Thursday morning saw the School hall packed with expectant (and non-expectant girls) and visitors. On the platform were seated our Trustees, Prof. Steele, Mr Lawrence M.A. (Headmaster of the Boys' Grammar School) and Miss White M.A., our Headmistress.*

The school dining room as it probably appeared in Queenie's day

23

The Chairman of Trustees, Mr Tatham, spoke on this occasion as did several other Trustees. Professor Steele distributed the prizes, saying a few words of congratulation to each recipient.

The ceremony concluded, the visitors and girls took lingering farewells of the various pupils, and hungry and excited ... adjourned to the dining room.

She does not hold back on her comments about exams, of which there seem to have been many. One assumes, in fact, that they were actually more like weekly tests. On 19 February she wrote *had two most cruel exams today, science and drawing. Mine are most frightful*. On 21 August she *had a most frightful, awful, Cruel, monstrocious German exam! I don't think I'll ever recover from it*. Queenie had a *dreadful day* on 19 October. She *had geography exam, then a fair German lesson. Middling English, then a cruel, cruel, Science Exam. Had game of tennis though to make up for it*.

Tennis appears to be one of her great delights in life and she seems to have been quite good. Whenever possible she and her friends had a game and she also umpired school teams. Tennis was one of the few activities available after school for boarders.

The original tennis courts with the Lodge in the background

24

Most boarders at any school can recall with delight the outings they had and Queenie's diary shows why. They were much appreciated diversions. Outings included walks, picnics and concerts. On 27 April Queenie

> *went out with Miss Hill and seven other girls tonight to see "The Arcadians". It was lovely. Liked Jack Meadows, Bobbie, Sombra and Eileen Cavanagh the best. Miss White saw us down there, but did not go in or come home with us.*

On 25 May the entry reads *Miss White let us see the cadet's procession in prep. tonight. We were so loyal – doing patriotic songs, etc., with Mrs. "O" as leader.* This event is also a rather quaint entry in the June 1914 Magazine

> *There was a rustling that seemed like a bustling*
> *Of merry crowds jostling at pitching and hustling,*
> *Small (?) feet were pattering, wooden shoes clattering,*
> *Little (?) hands clapping and little tongues chattering,*
> *And, like fowls in a farm-yard when barley is scattering*
> *Out came the children running*
> *To see the Torchlight Procession.*

Such was the state of affairs, with the exception of the *wooden shoes clattering* on the night of Monday, 25th May, when

> *we repaired from the School Hall and its musty books to enjoy a short interval on the West balcony, from which a remarkably good view of the Torchlight Procession could be obtained. We were charmed with the display of lights, and particularly the reflection in the river, as the procession crossed the Bremer Bridge on its way to the North Ipswich Reserve. The procession, however, did not wholly engross us as some touching scenes on the balcony itself claimed some of our attention, and sent us into "Fitz" (fits) of giggling'. We sang (?) the National Anthem and several patriotic songs and with three "boos" for lessons, cheerfully returned to the stuffy prep. rooms.*

One can't begin to imagine what the 'touching scenes' might have been! Perhaps something similar to a quaint account about another outing which the full-time boarders enjoyed.

> *On March 14th Mrs "O" took a party of us to Queen's Park, taking tea with us. We found infinite amusement in watching an interesting tableau – "A daylight Courtship". When to our astonishment, we saw a ring slipped on the young (??) maiden's finger, we concluded that such was not a scene for mortal eyes, and delicately turned in the opposite direction.*

On 3 June she went with *girls, in charge of Sixth form, to the Park where we had afternoon tea as a Picnic. Then went & watched the Town Club playing tennis.* Later that month, on 25 June, Queenie went to a Boys' Grammar Concert

> *in all the slosh-bosh and mud at night. Concert was very nice. Little Lord Fauntleroy is a darling. Got home about 11 o'clock, I think.*

The diary also captures events that were taking place at the school. In June the school was painted and the boarders had to move to different rooms temporarily. The diary records that the school also built new tennis courts in 1914, which must have been a delight to the tennis-loving Queenie.

Apart from her very frequent games of tennis Queenie spent much of her leisure time reading. She was a prolific reader and her tastes were quite eclectic.

Again some things never change. Dances and school formals are always the subject of much preparation and excitement and such was the case in 1914. On 31 August Queenie conveys *excitement over our evening-dresses* for the forthcoming balls and she says of the ball following the School Bazaar which Queenie went to with friends Phyllis, Roy and Myrtle Chalmers *Had a scrummy time. Danced nearly all night but with girls mostly.* There is evidence to suggest that Queenie was a bit of a 'flirt'. She certainly emerges as a 'character' full of life and with a great capacity for enjoyment.

And so Queenie's life at IGGS in 1914 is recounted in her diary –
the good times and not so good. Probably she would agree with her
anonymous contemporary whose poem *A Schoolgirl's Diary*
appeared in the June 1914 Magazine

> *Arose at 6. At 6.15*
> *Went down to do some History,*
> *And "War of Spanish Succession" found*
> *A most bewildering mystery.*
> *At 8, in tears I Latin tried,*
> *But find the verb I couldn't,*
> *And though at 9 the sun came out,*
> *Alas! the "Livy" wouldn't.*
> *From 9 to 10 a teacher cruel*
> *Shrieked at my Harmony,*
> *Declared my chords were tortured wails*
> *From Dante's "Purgatory".*
> *With 10 o'clock came Algebra,*
> *At 12 in desperation,*
> *Decided that a Sherlock Holmes*
> *Would weep at that equation!*
> *At 2 came "Mending;" Ah, alas!*
> *That hour of woe, I hate,*
> *For if "split skirts" the fashion are*
> *I'm truly up-to-date.*
> *At 3 came French – I conjugate*
> *"Je pleure" with much expression;*
> *And finally at 4 o'clock*
> *There came my Music-lesson.*
> *My Music-teacher's verdict fell,*
> *With satire highly flavoured,*
> *"She sees now why poor tortured Saul*
> *Cast javelins at David".*
> *Ah me! I find it hard to be*
> *A self-controlled and cool girl,*
> *Just when I've heard a grown-up say,*
> *"As happy as-------a SCHOOL-GIRL"!!!*

Page 92: 1914 Diary

"Had a lovely music lesson, short and sweet."

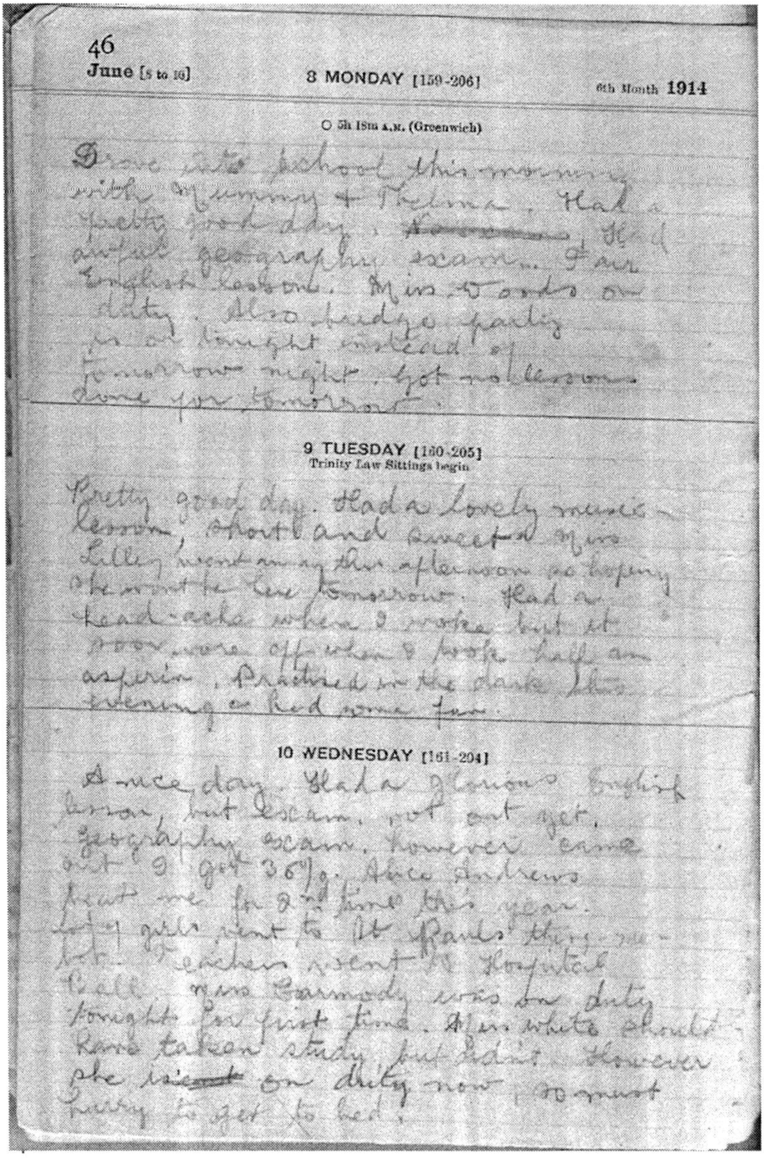

46
June [8 to 10] 8 MONDAY [159-206] 6th Month 1914

○ 5h 18m A.M. (Greenwich)

Drove into school this morning with Mummy + Thelma. Had a pretty good day. ~~[illegible]~~ Had awful geography exam. Fair English lessons. Miss Woods on duty. Also Madge's party is on tonight instead of tomorrow night. Got no lessons done for tomorrow.

9 TUESDAY [160-205]
Trinity Law Sittings begin

Pretty good day. Had a lovely music lesson, short and sweet. Miss Lilley went away this afternoon so hoping she won't be here tomorrow. Had a head-ache when I woke but it soon wore off when I took half an aspirin. Practised in the dark this evening & had some fun.

10 WEDNESDAY [161-204]

A nice day. Had a glorious English lesson, but exam. not out yet. Geography exam. however came out I got 36%. Alice Andrews beat me for 2nd time this year. Lot of girls went to St Pauls' [illegible]. Teachers went to Hospital Ball. Miss Carmody was on duty tonight for first time. Miss White should have taken study but didn't. However she is ~~[illegible]~~ on duty now, so must hurry to get to bed!

Queenie's Teachers

Staff and Boarders in 1917

Front row L to R: *Miss Hill (Art), Miss Gladys Hardwick (Music), Miss Irene Carmody (Geography), Mrs O'Connor (Matron), Miss Helen White (Headmistress), Miss Estelle Cribb (Maths), Miss Kathleen Lilley (English and French), Miss Charlotte Hodgens (French, Latin and Greek) and Miss Edna Cribb (Geology and Sport). The names of the girls are not known.*

There are constant references throughout the diary to teachers and other members of staff, and while the photo above was taken after Queenie left IGGS, some of her frequently mentioned teachers – Miss White, Miss Lilley, Miss Hill, Miss Carmody, Miss Estelle Cribb, Miss Edna Cribb – and the Matron, Mrs O'Connor, all appear in the photo above.

Miss Helen White was the School's Headmistress from 1906 until 1927. She was a graduate of Melbourne University and a good Classical and Mathematical Scholar, with a sound knowledge of French and German languages who brought to the position a great deal of professional knowledge.

29

Miss Helen White

She was a firm but kindly Head who for 22 years had a profound influence on the development of the School. She improved the life of the boarders for whom she tried to create more homely conditions.

She felt that the students should have closer links with the community and led by example. Through school garden parties and similar events, the girls were encouraged to raise money for charity.

Queenie refers to German lessons taught by Miss White in her sitting room, and it is noted in the December 1915 Magazine

> *Miss White invited us into the drawing room one Saturday to read Shakespeare's 'Julius Caesar', and we passed an enjoyable evening reading, for which we wish to thank her.*

Miss White features prominently in the diaries and she obviously played a significant role in the lives of the girls who had a great deal of respect for her. She was also highly regarded in the Ipswich community.

She showed great commitment to the School and frequently purchased items or undertook to pay for repairs she considered necessary from her own fairly meagre salary.

Other teachers mentioned include Miss Estelle Cribb who taught at the school for 35 years from 1903 until 1938. An inaugural pupil at Ipswich Girls' Grammar in 1892, she was one of the first women to receive an MA in Mathematics at Sydney University.

Miss Estelle Cribb

An excellent teacher, she was appointed Mathematics Mistress at IGGS and as she lived locally it was agreed that *She would not be a resident but would do her fair share of work with the girls after school.* This she most certainly did and the Magazines of the day are full of accounts of outings conducted by Miss Cribb. In retirement she was President of the Old Girls' Association for many years.[9]

Miss White's sitting room

31

*Miss Helen White and Miss Estelle Cribb on a
picnic at Berry's Lagoon*

Miss White and Miss Cribb led Bible Circles for the girls and organised many other activities. They both frequently took the girls on outings. Queenie notes on 3 June 1915

The only holiday in the year so made the most of it. About 10 am V and VI walked out to Kholo (6 miles away) with Miss Cribb. Rode part of the way on a bullock waggon. Paddled, etc., out there, and had one of the most ripping times I have ever had. The rest of the Lower School went for a motor-boat picnic this afternoon with Miss White.

Miss Kathleen Lilley taught at Ipswich Girls' Grammar from 1911 to 1923, prior to becoming Headmistress of Brisbane Girls Grammar. She and Miss White are referred to constantly throughout Queenie's writings and there is no doubt that they were respected as it is obvious that if they were on duty or imposed impositions, they were not to be treated lightly.

The diary refers to another staff member, Mrs Mortimore (Mrs Mort), and her resignation. This took place suddenly at Easter, after a stay of little more than 12 months at the school. Both the school magazine and Queenie's diary record that she *was presented with a silver ink stand.* Miss Carmody replaced Mrs Mortimore in April 1914. Queenie writes on 20 April *the new teacher, Miss Carmody from Rockhampton took us for hour-lesson geography.*

At the time of her retirement, Miss Irene Carmody was the school's longest serving teacher, teaching there until 1956. Known as 'Carm', she was a very strict disciplinarian who did not tolerate any misbehaviour but she was a totally committed teacher and encouraged girls to strive for academic success. Over the years Miss Carmody taught Arithmetic, Geography, History, Bookkeeping, Ancient History and Needlework. As Geography was the subject for which Queenie was awarded the prize in both her years at IGGS, Miss Carmody was probably 'tolerated'.

Miss Woods, who is also mentioned, joined the staff at the beginning of 1914 as a Sewing and Sports Mistress as well as a teacher of English in the lower school.

Basket Ball Team 1915
Standing: *Doris Woodward, Ida Sole, Lilian Adcock*
Sitting: *Miss Woods, Ida Adcock, Edith Ashley, Marcie McMahon and Madelen Hulbert*

33

She left to be married towards the end of 1914 and Queenie says on 23 September *had a look at Miss Wood's wedding presents* and *Put some "Good Luck" Coupons on Miss Wood's table for last night here.* The Magazine entry states

> *It was with great regret that we thought of parting with Miss Woods, our Sports Mistress, at Michaelmas. Under her guidance our sports have decidedly improved, and both last year and this we have made a good stand in the Sports Association matches. On behalf of the school, Miss White, in a happy little speech, presented Miss Woods with two handsome Wedgewood biscuit barrels which we hope will be useful in her new sphere of life. The Tennis and Basketball teams also presented her with "Keepsakes".*

These may well be the presents to which Queenie refers.

Miss Edna Cribb, who married Josiah Francis and was to become Lady Edna Francis, taught Gymnastics in Queenie's day and later became sports mistress and a teacher in the Lower School.

Tennis Team 1915

Standing: *Ethol Nichols, Hilda Withecombe*
Sitting: *Zoe Martin, Miss Edna Cribb and Alison Hooper*

Other teachers there in Queenie's day include Miss Pitts, a Science teacher, who commenced in 1913 and left at the end of 1915 to teach in Melbourne; Miss Francis who came in 1915 to teach Geology and Miss Hodgens, a Language teacher, remained at the school for several years.

Miss Hill is another lady who seemed to give a lot of time to the boarders as she is frequently referred to as having taken them on outings. There is also a reference in the June 1914 Magazine to her having started a Glee Club.

> *We are deeply indebted to Miss Hill for the formation of the Glee Club .... We enjoy the practices very much, and hope to make our debut with grand eclat when the time comes.*

On 25 March 1915 Queenie tells us

> *Tonight Hilda and I short sheeted Thelma's bed. Wouldn't let Thelma in the door. Miss Hill saw us but only laughed.*

Things weren't so good on 1 June, however, as

> *All of us were kept in by Miss Hill (pig!!!) for laughing at a great joke* and again on 24 August, *We three in this dorm. all got an impot – 200 hundred lines – from Miss Hill tonight, for making a row, so going to bed late.*

('We three' are Queenie and her friends Hilda Withecombe and Thelma Tritton.)

On Tuesday 3 November Queenie tells us *Miss Hill just came in to stop Hilda & me romping, but was a ducky darling about it.* It is hard to imagine this term being applied to Miss White, Miss Lilley or Miss Carmody!

The young boarding mistresses played a great part in the lives of boarders as they were the ones often on duty.

> *Miss Woods on duty & nearly forgot to put our lights out. So in consequence we had a good time. Miss Hill came in to stop our noise.*

On 3 February 1915 Queenie reports *New teacher Miss Hodgens was on duty.*

35

The inter-connecting walkway between the two buildings adjacent.

Perhaps the most frequently mentioned teacher is Miss Cadogan, Queenie's Music teacher who started teaching at IGGS at Easter 1913. As Queenie appears to have had an individual piano lesson with her on a regular daily basis, she seems to have played a fairly prominent part in the young girl's life. Queenie shares a lot of family news as on 8 September 1914 *Had a nice day. Had a beautiful music-lesson this morning. Told Miss Cadogan about Audrey.* It is impossible to know what the conversation was about but presumably Queenie was very proud of Audrey's success as a pianist so it could have related to that.

Miss Cadogan obviously tried to encourage Queenie who writes on 13 October 1914

Had a very lovely glorious music lesson this morning – best I ever had. Miss Cadogan informed me that I am to try for the Junior medal at Xmas.

Unfortunately on 21 October the entry reads *Had the most frightful music lesson I ever had since I've been here* but by 27 October *Had a very nice day. Had a pretty fair music lesson – I have forgiven Miss Cadogan now.* Thank goodness for that but did Miss Cadogan realise she had transgressed?

This side view of the old buildings is labelled 'Studio with my dorm above' in a photo from Queenie's era.
(Note this is the backdrop to the photo of Queenie taken at IGGS.)

Queenie, in fact, did not try for the Junior medal as on 1 December writes *Think I will get out of my Medal piece, if I can.* Queenie was in luck as on 4 December *Miss Cadogan relieved my mind telling me I had no chance for the Medal* and then says of the exam day *made a fool of myself at exam* and on 8 December writes *Had a lovely music lesson. Miss Cadogan laughed at my mistakes in music exam.*

Miss Cadogan was herself a pianist of some note, it would appear, as there are a number of references to recitals and performances, both public and for the entertainment of the girls. On 16 June 1915 Queenie writes

Eileen and I went down and heard Miss Cadogan playing some glorious pieces before study.

She left IGGS six months after Queenie and the 1916 Magazine records

We said "good-bye" to Miss Cadogan who has gone to join her mother in England. Before leaving, Miss Cadogan was presented by the pupils with a silver purse in recognition of the regard in which she was held.

Another teacher who is mentioned in passing is Mr Jones – he is actually mentioned mostly for his absence. On 30 April 1914 Queenie tells *Had no book-keeping lesson, as teacher, Mr. Jones did not turn up,* and in November of that year: *Mr. Jones didn't turn up for book-keeping, so Thelma & I had lessons to ourselves.*

However most of the book-keeping lessons she did have met with her approval as on 27 August 1914 *Had a most beautiful book-keeping lesson.* The book-keeping prize which Queenie won at the end of 1914 was donated by a Mr Jones – presumably this teacher.

Miss Kennedy mentions in *The First One Hundred Years* that some thought was being given at this time to the introduction of what were to become the Commercial subjects, but it didn't happen until some time later.[10] As this seems to be a very small class – Queenie and Thelma – and Mr Jones would seem to be an 'outside' teacher perhaps the girls had private lessons.

On 13 September 1915 Queenie writes

> *Saw, and got a glorious smile from, Mr Jones, our old Book-keeping teacher in Dinmore Station.*

One assumes that 'old' can be interpreted as 'former', as a glorious smile from an old man would be unlikely to have had much appeal for the delightfully flirtatious Queenie.

Another staff member who attracts frequent mention is the Matron, Mrs O'Connor. She seems to have been a much-loved Matron which was not necessarily 'the norm' in boarding schools. She was very actively involved with the girls in many of their activities. This was the lady who worked tirelessly for the war effort and whose contribution to various charities, Allies' Markets and so forth is referred to by Queenie and well documented in the Magazines.

One lovely entry of Queenie's on 6 May 1915 says

> *Mrs O had something on this afternoon for the Belgiums (sic), but, of course, we weren't in it. Held meeting at dinner time about Bazaar.*

What Mrs O'Connor 'had' and why 'we weren't in it' we shall never know but it is obvious that the school was used extensively for the war efforts undertaken by the Matron.

In *The First One Hundred Years* we read that at the 1915 Speech Day

> *Mrs O'Connor thanked the Trustees for allowing her to do patriotic work outside the School and for the use of the grounds for the Allies' Markets.*

Two years later, however, Mrs O *was told not to take so much interest in matters outside her school duties* which may well have been the reason for her resignation in September 1917.[11]

Some years later the Brisbane Branch of the Old Girls Association initiated 'The Mrs O'Connor Memorial Prize for Services in the Boarding School' – an award which is still presented annually at Speech Night.

A photo from Queenie's memorabilia of a school outing

Page 101: 1914 Diary

Hilda & I just short-sheeted Thelma's bed.

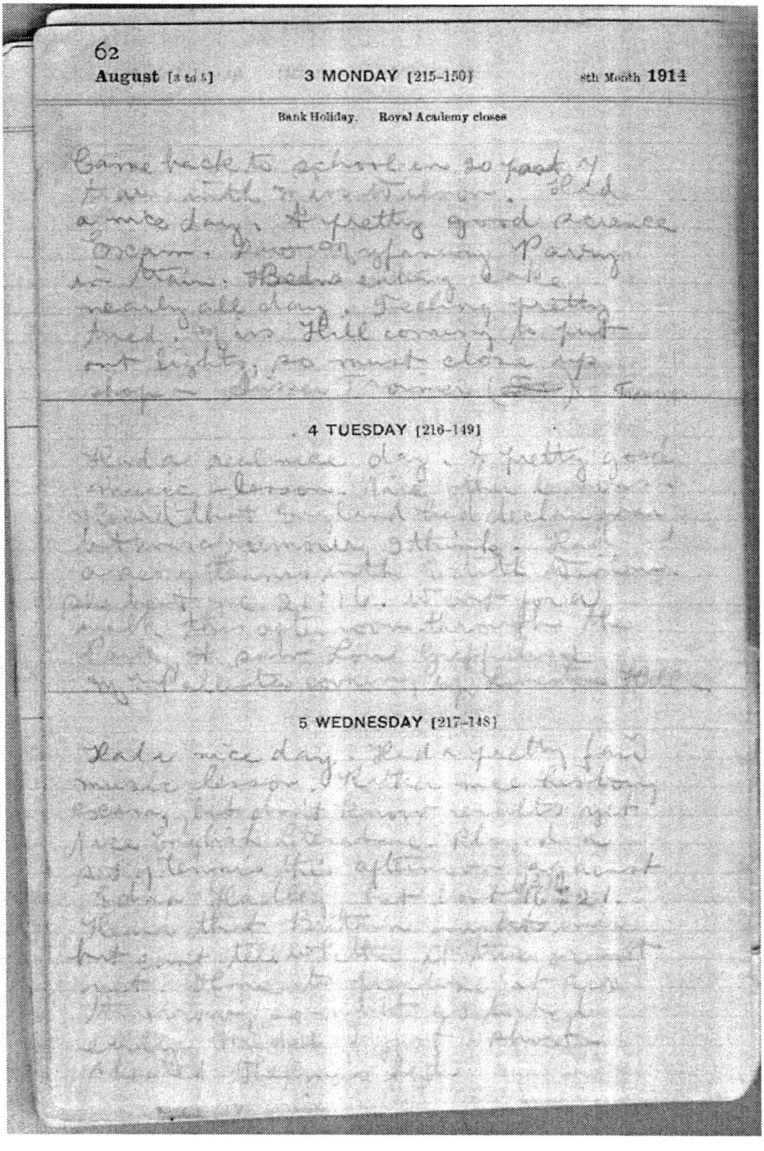

62

August [3 to 5] 3 MONDAY [215-150] 8th Month 1914

Bank Holiday. Royal Academy closes

4 TUESDAY [216-149]

5 WEDNESDAY [217-148]

Queenie's Friends

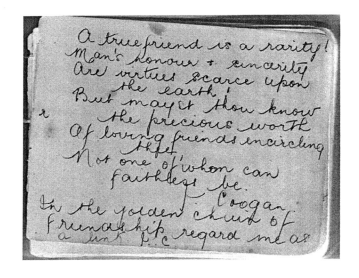

A true friend is a rarity!

Man's honour and sincerity

Are virtues scarce upon the earth!

But mayst thou know the precious worth

Of loving friends encircling thee,

No one of whom can faithless be.

J. Coogan

In the golden chain of friendship regard me as a link

J.C.

Not surprisingly the diary pages are full of stories of Queenie's activities with her close friends. There are many young people mentioned in her writings. Some of them are her cousins and neighbours at Redbank Plains and others family friends, but a significant number of them are her classmates and boarding friends.

One girl who seems to have been a close family friend and also a school friend was (Margaret) **Phyllis Wilson** who was born on 26 January 1899. She attended IGGS from 3 February 1913 until 9 December 1915 as a day girl. Her father was A Wilson and the family lived in Roderick Street.

In the very first week of the 1914 diary the Jones and Wilson families are at Stradbroke Island and spent quite some time together through the summer. On 31 January she writes

> *Came into town in morning. Had dinner at Wilson's and then went to Grammar School with Mummy and Roy. Coming back watched games of bowls and tennis. At night went to Martoo's pictures with Phyllis and Roy. Staying at Wilson's till Monday.*

On 1 February she writes *Went to church in morning. Sunday school with Phil in the afternoon and then we both went up into the Park.* Roy is Roy Wilson, presumably Phyllis's brother.

There are frequent references to a 'Miss Wilson' (an older sister or perhaps an aunt?) as on 9 February *Heard all about Miss Wilson's party from Phyllis.* There was obviously a great deal of coming and going between the two families. On 13 February Queenie notes *Daddy called for me in the afternoon and drove Phyllis and me down town.*

On 15 October 1914 Queenie writes *Had a most frightful day – Horrible. Heard that little Frances Wilson was dead. Got an awful shock* and on 19 October notes *Phyllis came back to school,* presumably having been absent because of her little sister's death.

There seems to be a deterioration in the friendship after this though certainly no reason can be deduced through the diary entries. On 17 December 1914 Queenie got *a 'surprising' letter from Miss Wilson* and on 5 February 1915 she notes *Mummy called at Wilson's this afternoon for an explanation about Southport.*

There are a number of references about Phyllis in the 1915 diary both written and hinted at which are certainly different in sentiment from those of the earlier diary as on 1 May *Phyllis got offended at something or other* and on 21 June *I was just told that Phyllis spoke to me today but I didn't hear her, so I suppose she's offended* and on 6 August *Saw "my darling" (otherwise Phyllis) in town, and she gave me a beaming smile (I don't think).* Goodness knows what happened to cause this apparent rift which seems to have been between the two families and not just the girls.

For the most part her comments about her friends are quite innocuous as on 1 March 1914

> *Two of my persimmons were ripe. Jessie Coogan had one, (at least, I gave it to Jessie and all the kids had bite). Played a set of tennis with Jessie Coogan, Laura Brazier and Ruth George. Ruth and I were beaten 6 games to 5.*

There are constant references to tennis games in which Jessie Coogan features very frequently.

Some of her entries reveal normal school-girls' mischief as you have already read. On 19 March 1914 she admits *Been talking to Jessie Elsworthy at the window for the last half hour, scared Miss Lilley will come round, so better shut up* and again on 23 March *Had a good talk to Jessie Elsworthy in her room where a couple of teachers nearly saw me.* Behaviour in dormitories was obviously rigorously controlled. On 18 August 1915 *Came upstairs early with Eileen (without permission) and lay on her bed until 5.45.*

One delightful entry is on 20 May 1914 *Hilda & I were shown by Miss Woods this morning how to walk down stairs.* The mind can just conjure up this scene and there will be many boarders of more recent years who will recall being admonished for hurtling down the stairs!

On 22 May 1915 we learn of another misdemeanour *Dodged taking exercise this afternoon. Sat down near the swings with Jessie Coogan and Thelma Graham,* while on 5 August she tells us *Hilda & I just short-sheeted Thelma's bed.* There are numerous references to squabbles such as 31 March 1914 *Am rowing with Thelma all the time I'm writing* and 19 October 1915 *Hilda and Eileen are at daggers, so I must try to clear up things if possible.*

On 15 June 1915

*there was a Big bust up between V and VI dorms.
Mis White came on the scene and V dorm had to
do study for an hour extra*

and on 19 November

*We had to defend our room against Lower V
today and tonight. Had great sport, only other
kids got an imposition from Carm.*

Her great friend at IGGS in 1914 was **Thelma Tritton**. Born on
8 February 1899, Thelma attended Ipswich Girls' Grammar School
from 23 July 1913 until 12 December 1914. Her father was J Tritton
of the Sportsman's Hotel in Leichhardt Street, Brisbane. On 12 April
1915 Queenie writes that she was 'aghast' that Thelma was not
coming back to school. The friendship continued through
correspondence and Thelma stayed at 'Oakleigh' from 25 February
1915 until 1 March 1915. Thelma, like many others, recorded tradi-
tional messages in Queenie's autograph book.

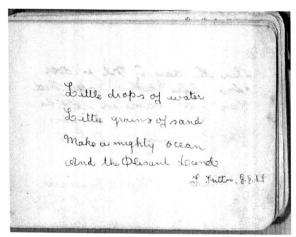

Thelma Tritton's autograph

There is a happy ending to Queenie's school days as her great
friend from the previous year Thelma Tritton has remained loyal.
On 20 November *Got a letter from Thelma wishing me luck in the
Junior.*

Another very good friend was **Hilda Withecombe**. Born on 18 March 1899, she attended Ipswich Girls' Grammar from 3 February 1913 to 12 December 1917. Her father was Mr Withecombe Esq. of Dixon Street, Wooloowin. She passed Junior in 1915 and Senior in 1917. She was awarded an Old Girls' Scholarship to attend University and completed a Bachelor of Arts in 1921. She later married Albert Axon and became Lady Axon when her husband was awarded a knighthood. In 1914 Queenie, Thelma and Hilda shared a dormitory.

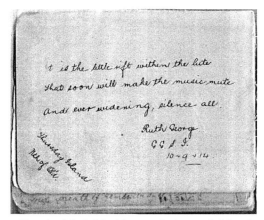

*It is the little rift
within the lute
That soon will make
the music mute
And ever widening,
silence all.
Ruth George
G.G.S.I.
10 - 9 - 14*

Note the delightful address in the bottom left hand corner:

Ruth George (or Blanche Evelyn Ruth George), born 13 March 1900, came from Thursday Island. She attended IGGS from 5 March 1914 until 13 December 1916, sitting for the Junior Examination in 1916. She attended the school on an Old Girls' Scholarship, and later completed a Bachelor of Arts in Queensland. Ruth George became a stalwart of the Brisbane Branch of the Old Girls' Association and worked tirelessly to raise funds for the Reference Library.

Marjorie Caroline Barnett, born 18 February 1897, she attended IGGS from 24 July 1911 until 9 December 1915 and sat for her Junior. Her father was K Barnett of Nicholas Street. Marjorie became a Nursing Sister at Ipswich General Hospital, and eventually its Deputy Matron. The Nurses Home attached to the hospital, built in 1966, bears her name. Queenie's friendship with Marjorie continued beyond their years at IGGS.

One of the difficulties in tracing these girls is that Queenie did not usually give them surnames and many of them had first names in common. Several of them were called by 'nick names' such as 'Girlie' Foote and others seemed to attend school intermittently. Where possible we have included some information about the girls mentioned.

Jessie Coogan, born 7 April 1899, was the daughter of PJ Coogan from Gayndah. She attended Ipswich Girls' Grammar School from 24 February 1913 until 9 December 1915. She sat for her Junior in 1915.

Laura Victoria Brazier, born 22 February 1900, attended Ipswich Girls' Grammar School from 10 February 1914 until 13 December 1916. Her father was J Brazier of Jandowie.

Jessie Elsworthy, born 17 September 1900, was the daughter of F Elsworthy from Mackay. She attended Ipswich Girls' Grammar School from 1 February 1914 until 22 June 1916.

Thelma Graham, born 1 January 1898, came from a property, 'Boondooma' near Wandai. Her father was A Graham. Thelma was at the school from 7 February 1914 until 12 December 1914.

Margaret Gillies, born 12 October 1899, was the daughter of P Gillies Esq. who lived at 'Plain View Park', Dalby. She attended Ipswich Girls' Grammar School from 19 April 1913 until 13 December 1916. Her sketch in Queenie's diary is reproduced on the left.

Miriam Luck, born 20 August 1900, came from 'Balclutha' at Cambooya, the property of her father H E Luck. She attended Ipswich Girls' Grammar School from 6 February 1914 until 13 December 1916. School records state that she was a 'scholar new conditions' which presumably refers to a type of scholarship.

This group of girls were at IGGS the year before Queenie started but their style of dress and appearance would have been the same in her day.

Doris Winifred Woodward, born 29 May 1900, was the daughter of FG Woodward and attended Ipswich Girls' Grammar School from 31 January 1914 until 13 December 1916.

Evelyn Horton, born 24 July 1899, was the daughter of J Horton from Engelsburg. (Engelsburg was the name for Kalbar before World War I when anti-German sentiment forced the district to change its name.) Evelyn enrolled at Ipswich Girls' Grammar School in 1913 and re-enrolled in 1917. She passed Junior in 1915 and Senior in 1917.

Alice Andrews, born 15 September 1898, came from Tallebudgera. Her father was C Andrews. She attended Ipswich Girls' Grammar School from 5 February 1913 until 12 December 1914.

Kathleen Mary Harsant, born 10 November 1897, was the daughter of W Harsant of Fassifern. She attended Ipswich Girls' Grammar School from 5 February 1911 until 14 December 1915 and passed Junior in 1913 and Senior in 1915.

Dorothy Creaser, born 16 December 1900, was the daughter of A Creaser of Brisbane. She attended Ipswich Girls' Grammar School from 3 February 1913 until 13 December 1916, passing Junior in 1916. It is known that she died in 1981 in York, England.

Muriel Collins, born 10 August 1898, attended Ipswich Girls' Grammar School from Rosewood from 20 April 1914 until 13 December 1916.

Esther Foote, born 3 February 1901, attended IGGS from 5 February 1911 until 13 December 1916. Her father was H Foote Esq. of Thorn Street and she sat Junior in 1916.

Edith Margaret Winlaw, born 20 September 1898, was the daughter of JW Winlaw of Woodend, Ipswich. She attended Ipswich Girls' Grammar School from 19 July 1913 until 7 May 1915. She completed Junior in 1915 to 1918 and a Bachelor of Arts in 1922. School records show she was on a Sacrificer Scholarship to apply for teaching work.

Dorothy McGill, born 18 June 1897, was a day girl, whose father was JW McGill of Warwick Road, Ipswich. She attended Ipswich Girls' Grammar School from 31 January 1914 until 9 December 1915, passing Queensland Junior in 1915.

Ida Adcock, born 15 January 1898, was the daughter of JH Adcock of Toowoomba. She attended Ipswich Girls' Grammar School from 20 April 1914 until 9 September 1915.

Ethel Nicols, born 13 May 1898, was the daughter of A Nichols Esq. from Chillagoe. She attended Ipswich Girls' Grammar School from 1 February 1915 until 13 December 1917. She completed Queensland Junior in 1915 and Senior in 1917.

Jean Nathale Cramond, born 18 January 1898, came from Toowoomba, the daughter of D Cramond. She enrolled at Ipswich Girls' Grammar School from 1 February 1915 until 13 December 1916.

(Lillian) Jessie Horton, born 29 October 1897, was the daughter of T Horton and attended Ipswich Girls' Grammar School from 3 February 1912 until December 1913.

Zoe Estelle Martin, born 7 July 1987, was the daughter of G Martin of Toowoomba. She attended Ipswich Girls' Grammar School from 5 February 1912 to 12 December 1917. She completed Junior in 1914, Senior in 1916 and 1917 and a Bachelor of Arts in 1921. She became Headmistress of Newcastle Anglican Grammar School.

Lillah Taylor, born 25 November 1901, was the daughter of E Taylor of Killarney. She attended Ipswich Girls' Grammar School from 8 February 1915 until 5 December 1918. She passed Junior in 1916 and Senior in 1918.

Queenie Alice Lilian Morgan, born 18 May 1897, lived on Denmark Hill, Ipswich. The daughter of S Morgan she attended Ipswich Girls' Grammar School from 18 March 1915 until 9 December 1915.

Marjorie Agnes Hall, born 20 September 1902, was the daughter of T Hall of East Ipswich. She attended Ipswich Girls' Grammar School from 3 February 1912 until 5 December 1918, completing Queensland Junior in 1918.

Edith England, born 1 July 1899, was the daughter of J England of Boonah. She attended Ipswich Girls' Grammar School from 3 February 1913 until 13 December 1916. A prolific writer while at school, she became a poet of some note, and the school honours her by awarding the EM England Poetry prize each year at Speech Night.

This sketch of a horse from Queenie's autograph book is signed EME of Boonah, dated 18 June 1914.

49

Page 180: 1915 Diary

"Heard that 4000 soldiers from Enoggera were having a route march to Ipswich today."

50

Queenie's War

Ipswich Girls' Grammar School did not live in isolation and the impact of world events such as World War I was felt, even though its declaration was greeted with scepticism by Queenie. On 4 August 1914 she writes *heard that England had declared war. But was a rumour, I think.* The following day she records *heard that Britain was at war but can't tell whether it's true or not yet.* By 6 August the rumour appears to be confirmed and she writes *heard that the English fleet had "bottled up" the German fleet.* Later, on 17 August, she receives news of *the great war being fought.*

As well as references to special war effort functions Queenie tells of family friends such as Harold Younger joining up and her diary, on 28 December 1914, records her saying goodbye as he went off to war.

At IGGS, the girls were encouraged to work for the war effort by the staff, in particular the Headmistress Miss White and the Matron Mrs O'Connor. The latter devoted a great deal of time to fundraising.

School activities reflected that Australia was at war. On 31 August 1914 Queenie *made some button-holes in a kit bag for the soldiers this afternoon.* As part of their school work the girls had to write essays on patriotism. On 23 September 1914 Queenie's friend Hilda Withecombe went to a *Patriotic concert in town. Mrs O. went down town dressed all in red, white & blue – hideous.*

Ipswich itself was gripped by patriotic fervour. Many Ipswich men enlisted and it is recorded that when a 'patriotic meeting' was held in the Town Hall the attendance was so great that an overflow meeting had to be held outside.[12]

Branches of the Red Cross were formed, patriotic parades and concerts held, and recruiting parades and rallies were a regular part of the life of the town.

By 1915, World War I was having a greater impact on the school and the wider community as Queenie's diary records casualties amongst her acquaintances. On 5 May Queenie has

heard there is a big casualty list of Queenslanders today, but haven't seen it yet. Only know that the Rev. Robertson's son was killed in action. Dreadful. I feel as if I'd like to howl, which I will do if anyone I know is killed.

The next day the names are known as Queenie writes *terribly long list of deaths today, two Ipswich men – Robertson and Roberts among them.* This was indeed the case as Major S Robertson and Lt T Roberts both died in the first days of the Gallipoli campaign.

More of Queenie's friends were signing up with the diary recording that Allen and George Foote joined up at Enoggera in August 1915. Local men presumably known to Queenie are mentioned: George Pottinger and Mr Nash are recorded as being killed at the Dardanelles, while she notes that Joe Coogan was injured there. (One assumes Joe was related to Jessie Coogan who features in the notes about her friends.)

On 15 May Queenie records *It rained hard nearly all afternoon. I had some music and painting and also did a lot of knitting for soldiers* and on 2 October she writes *Got a "Rising*
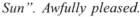
Sun". Awfully pleased.

School life was increasingly affected by the war. The Editorial in the June 1915 Magazine states *Most of us devote some time to working for our soldiers, and a donation is sent every month from the School to the local branch of the Red Cross.*

In December we read

Almost everyone has taken some part in the patriotic work of the town and in this we have always had the assistance of our indefatigable Matron.

A further entry tells us

On March 31ˢᵗ, Mrs O'Connor took a party of girls to see a display of Red Cross work at Cribb and Foote's. The people of Ipswich have been busily working for the soldiers, and a large supply of caps, socks, mittens etc., were exhibited. Mrs O'Connor takes particular interest in the Belgians.

This interest was obviously passed on to the girls because the same Magazine entry tells us that the IV Form performed a play entitled 'Lady Jane' and an admission fee of ½d or 1d was charged. *The proceeds, amounting to a few shillings, were given to the Belgian Relief Fund.*

In May IGGS was busy preparing for the Allies Market to raise money for those serving abroad.

We would like to take the opportunity of wishing Mrs O'Connor every success for her "Allies Market", and hope that a very large sum of money will be raised for the wounded soldiers of our own dear Australia.

The Magazine tells us

The "Allies Market" which was held on June 19ᵗʰ, was to many of us "the day" of the second term. The School grounds were quite transformed, the old tennis courts being decorated with innumerable flags and fancy stalls. The paddock adjoining the grounds was also looking quite gay. A small merry-go-round was set up, and there were various kinds of amusements.

From the December 1915 Magazine we learn

*The annual Bazaar, in aid of charities, was held
on October 16th. A new feature of the Bazaar
was that the stallholders all wore fancy costumes,
the gay colours of which were a distinct improve-
ment on the formerly monotonous white.*

There follows a full page of descriptions about the contents or activities
of each stall.

*The Ice Cream, Fruit Salad was a great centre
of attraction especially to "ye smalle boye" and
Miss Lilley and Miss Carmody – assisted by a
troupe of "Follies"– had quite a strenuous time.*

Queenie reports on 10 November

*Went to a Debating meeting in shed this after-
noon. Subject, "Should Conscription be put into
force during the War". Against it, won. I voted
differently.*

Queenie's diaries also refer to reading war stories after school,
which most likely were the accounts of the war reported in *The
Queensland Times* and contemporary magazines.

In her 1915 diary Queenie penned the following lines, similar to the many patriotic songs of the time:

We have watched you playing cricket
And every kind of game.
At football, golf and polo,
You men have made your name.
But now your country calls you,
To play your part in war,
And no matter what befalls you
We shall love you all the more.
So come and join the forces,
As your fathers did before.

Chorus
Oh, we don't want to lose you,
But we think you ought to go.
For your King and your country,
Both need you so.
We shall want you and miss you,
But with all our might and main,
We shall cheer you, thank you, kiss you,
When you come back again.

It's easy for us women
To stay at home and shout
But remember there's a duty
To the men who first went out.
The odds against that handful
Were nearly four to one
And we cannot rest until
It's man to man and gun for gun!
And every woman's duty
Is to see that duty done.

Page 139: 1915 Diary

"Hate lessons now that the holidays have ended."

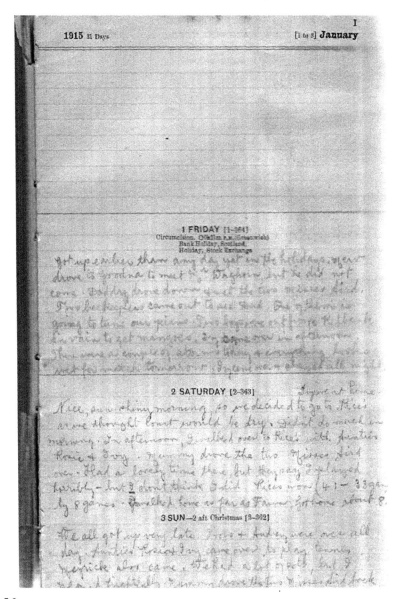

Queenie's School in 1915

The gates of IGGS in Queen Victoria Parade, with the Lodge on the left and the still familiar jacaranda and Moreton Bay figs in the driveway.

By 1915 Queenie is in her final year at Ipswich Girls' Grammar School, in Form V. The diary covers the school year from 1 February until 9 December 1915, her last day of school.

The school year diary begins with a comment shared by many students (and possibly teachers) over the years

> *First day at school this year. Didn't like it extra much. Ever so many new girls. Hate lessons now that the holidays have ended.*

The diary continues in much the same vein as her 1914 volume with its candid accounts of teachers, her workload and her fellow pupils. The exaggeration you would now be familiar with continues in 1915.

On 17 February Queenie writes *Got millions of lessons to do tonight* and on 25 August she was *nearly killed with lessons for tomorrow.* On 24 February she had *the most awful Algebra exam I ever even dreamt of or heard about. I got 13, and not lowest either.*

On 4 August, Queenie *had the most frightful Algebra Exam I have ever seen (and got 8). I did not imagine that anything could be so awful.* Things were not all bad in Mathematics as on 11 August she had a *Very nice algebra lesson. Then had an extra good Arithmetic lesson. Miss Carmody evidently thinks I'm not the worst in the class after all.* History was not spared criticism as 17 November provided *one of the rottenest History lessons we've ever had.*

There are other 'tragedies' in this young life. She is *made* to walk round for exercise, kept in for laughing in Prep and on 27 April *Lost two lead pencils, so am nigh stony broke.*

The accounts of everyday activities continue to give an insight into her school life. On 1 June she records *Zoe Martin took us for dumb-bells, as Miss Woods is away, so didn't do much but fool.* It was ever thus!!

An exercise in calisthenics

The dumb-bells referred to were part of the calisthenics exercises regularly undertaken. An early prospectus states that *calisthenics exercises such as Indian club swinging, dumbells &c are practised for a quarter-of-an-hour daily under the guidance of an experienced teacher.*

The play-shed, one of the original buildings

These were often held in the play-shed as were a number of extra-curricular activities. Walking was another 'regular activity' which was not popular if Queenie's comments are any indication. On 23 March she comments *Practised or pretended to this afternoon while others went for a walk.* One senses that piano practice was the lesser of two evils.

The start of her last semester brought the now familiar groans
> *Got up real early and drove down to Goodna with Dad and back to school by train. Oh! hateful, hateful!! Got on alright in lessons, and had two preparations as chucked music now. Helped Jessie unpack, read, eat chocolate, and broke several rules this afternoon. To think of it being first day after Mid-winter holidays, Oh! horrible, horrible!!*

Queenie's Fifth Form companions were obviously a 'militant' group who felt entitled to their rights. They register several complaints in the June 1915 Magazine
> *Notice is hereby given that our form-room is not a public highway during lessons and study time.*

59

For some unknown reason we have been deprived of the right to our form-room on Thursday and Friday afternoons. Could someone please enlighten us upon this subject.

The dogs of Ipswich make a great mistake in thinking that Fifth Form is a retreat for stray dogs. They have doubtless found out their mistake now, for they are generally forced to retreat more quickly than they enter.

Queenie continued to enjoy her tennis playing but the same cannot be said about basketball. On 15 September she complains *Then donned a Basket Ball rigout this afternoon, and we played our first match. We played well, but were defeated – 43 to 9, by Lower V. I was defender, and oh! I never wish to see the game again as long as I live. I fell over twice and as the consequence, I have my knee bandaged up, and my stockings in holes.*

Her comments on teachers continue to be frank. She writes on 16 February 1915 *Miss Lilley got into one of her little tempers in English this morning.*

This photo, taken in 1926, is of the 'new' tennis courts about which Queenie was so pleased. These are the courts adjacent to Chermside Road.

On 4 March

Miss White got real worked up in German and forgot the time, and went on another quarter-of-an-hour. Had a bonser time. So in consequence had a short English lesson.

On 25 August Miss Lilley had *the biggest "little outbreak" she has had for ever so long.* The delights of boarding continue to be treats and outings. Queenie records that 31 March

was a great day. Most marvellous of all the delights, all the school had usual study, and then went out into the garden in the moonlight. Also, not by any means least, we all went over to the tuckshop and invested in lollies and fruit. Had a great feast on the turf in the moonlight. Feeling awfully excited.

The tuckshop referred to was a recently new attraction for the boarders and the start of a tradition of buying snacks at the Fiveways shop which survives to this day. The June 1914 Magazine tells us

Great excitement prevails when a party of happy girls visit the 'tuck' shop – a comparatively new institution. Notwithstanding the limited space allowed for the accommodation of customers, the proud possessor of the small establishment generally finds himself confined in some corner. The poor man has no chance to show his wares, but we supply that deficiency fairly well.

The final entries refer the Junior examination papers and the associated traumas.

Memorable day today alright. Our Junior started. Had "Compulsory" in morning, which I perhaps passed in and English in the afternoon, which I certainly failed in. It was a most abominable paper. Didn't get a bit nervous or flurried, thank goodness!!

The next few days are full of exam references until on 20 November she writes *Had a horrid German Exam this morning, but thank goodness! it's the last of my Junior subjects.*

It was obviously a time for celebration and she tells us on 2 December

> *This afternoon Miss White took all Junior and Senior examinees of both Boys' and Girls' School, to a spread in Whitehouses [Café in Nicholas Street Ipswich]. We had a bonser time.*

She wasn't as happy a week later

> *Miss White made me go to "Breaking-Up" at Boys' Grammar, although I didn't want to. We all went up in cabs. Met Mum and Merv there. Then, after afternoon tea, we drove home together. I got pretty right once I started. Last day's school.*

Queenie passed all five Junior Public Examination subjects for which she sat: History of England, Geography, English, German and Arithmetic. She is also in the 1915 Prize Lists, being awarded the prize for Geography. The June 1916 Magazine gives an account of Queenie's last Prize Giving

> *On December 10th of last year our "breaking-up" ceremony was held in conjunction with the Boys' Grammar School.*

> *One feature of the "breaking-up" was the absence of prizes. Both our prizes and those of the boys, although they had been ordered early in the year, did not arrive from England in time. This was a keen disappointment to both boys and girls, but it was the fortune of war and we had to resign ourselves to it. Instead of prizes, ornamental cards were distributed, on which were written the prizes to which the bearer was entitled.*

1914
Diary

Thursday 1
Went over to Stradbroke @ 8.30am. Had two bathes. Ivy and I had a really good rest in a tree over the water. Went fern-hunting. Mosquitoes nearly ate us. Came home @ 4pm. Nance W., Ivy and I went to Station at night. Saw F. Gibson in distance. Cecil R., Roy G., Ivy and I played cards until nearly 10 o'clock. Got a bet on, of an ice cream, to keep diary full, with C. Robinson, so keep it up. (21/12/14 - and won it)

Friday 2
Went for a bathe. Then Audrey and I went shopping. After dinner we had word competitions. I won the first and Cecil R. won the second. While Mum, Ivy and Audrey went to main beach, I went for a walk, met Cecil R. and Miss Wilson and had a rest. Miss Nimmo and Muriel Ford were with us. I went to station with Wilsons at night. Had a good concert afterwards.

Saturday 3
Went to see Ivy and friends off at 7 am Came home and cleaned shoes etc.. Miss Adsett visited us and had lunch here. Mr and Mrs Exton arrived. Had dinner in bedroom. Went for a bathe. Rested all the afternoon in bedroom. Played cards, etc. I went for a read on beach. We all went down town at night.

Sunday 4
Got up late, had breakfast and went for a bathe. Packed our luggage all the afternoon. Went to Jackson's. Came home by the beach, and had tea at Pohlman's. Had a talk to Barney Boulton. Went to bed as soon as we came home.

Monday 5
Caught the 7 am train and arrived at home for dinner. Unpacked our luggage all the afternoon. Auntie Clare drove over in the afternoon and took Audrey home with her. I read after that until tea time. Merv then rode over to the farm and brought Audrey home. Daddy went over to school at night. I stayed up and read. The others went to bed early.

Tuesday 6

Got up late. Practised music and read all morning. Same in the afternoon. Ivors came over from the farm with Daddy and Audrey in the morning and Merv took her home at night. After tea Lewis Griffiths came over and stayed until ten o'clock. I finished reading "Jane Eyre". Audrey and I went to bed fairly late.

Wednesday 7

Got up early and helped Mummy with washing, etc. all the morning. Daddy went to Ipswich. Audrey went as far as farm with him and stayed all day. Merv went to Goodna for the mail. Washed all the afternoon until about 4 o'clock. Then Vera and Daisy came over and stayed until 5.30pm. After tea, Ma came over and stayed about an hour. Ivy returned home from Brisbane and brought Merv some "Buffalo Bill" stories. We stayed up reading them until pretty late. It was Mummy's birthday.

Thursday 8

I got up and got breakfast for Daddy and the others. Mummy stayed in bed as she was not well. I ironed all the morning. After dinner I had a rest and then went on ironing. Morgan came over about sundown to play tennis. He stayed until about 9.30pm playing cards. Merv and Daddy were printing all the afternoon. Received letter saying my resignation from Ed. Dept. was accepted.

Friday 9

Didn't do much all morning. Mummy ironed. Audrey went over to Farm. Ivy brought her back with Audrey Barns and Thelma Macdonald. Merv and Dad went to Goodna. Mr Barram came for bee goods. After dinner, I took kiddies home and stayed with Ivy all the afternoon as Ma and Auntie Clare went to Brisbane. Auntie Clare drove me home about dark. I had a practice and am now going to bed. Signs of a storm.

Saturday 10

Got up very late. My face was swollen all the morning. Must have been bitten by something. Was working all day. Cleaned one harness room entirely. Swept all the yards, as well as odd jobs. A thunderstorm in the afternoon. Ma came over at night and took Audrey home with her. We all went to bed pretty early.

Sunday 11

Got up and did all the work early, as Mummy stayed in bed. Merv went over and brought Audrey home. Very hot. Meyrick J., Ivy and Auntie Clare and Mr Parker (with grapes) came in the afternoon.

Monday 12

Raining all day. Read Shakespeare's "Othello" all morning. Sorted music, read and fooled around all the afternoon. While Mummy read out to Audrey and Merv, I stayed up and fooled about drawing etc. and then went to bed.

Tuesday 13

Tremendous storm about 3 o'clock this morning. It has been showery all day. Mummy and I washed all morning. I read out to Audrey this afternoon, also washed back verandah. There is a good deal of thunder and lightning just now but very little rain. I think we will have some though. I am now going to bed at 9.30pm.

Wednesday 14

I ironed all the morning. Gathered mangoes after dinner. As Daddy and Merv had gone to Brisbane, Mummy, Audrey and I went over to the farm about 3 o'clock. Alma, with her three kiddies, were there. It has been very cloudy and dull all day, but no rain has fallen. Auntie Clare went to Ipswich by train. Mummy received a letter from Miss Wilson saying she would be here tomorrow. It is just striking 9 o'clock. I am going to bed.

Thursday 15

Miss Wilson arrived here. Daddy and Audrey went to meet her. In the afternoon, Mrs, Miss, May, Eric and Vera Hebden came over. They went home about dark. Perce and Lel were over at night, had music, etc. and went home at 10.30pm. They were also over in the morning to get a loan of Dad's gun. Auntie Clare was over for a long time, dyeing a dress.

Friday 16

Practised in morning. In the afternoon I went over for my music lesson and had singing after. Mum, Audrey and Miss Wilson went out visiting to the village. While Vera and I were coming home (Vera came part of the way for a walk), the others caught up and we all went over to the Farm, and stayed for a while. Ate mangoes and peaches when we got home. I prepared to go to Brisbane.

Saturday 17

Went down to Brisbane by 10 am train with Auntie Clare and Ivy. Saw Auntie Clare off, by the "Hyarra", bound for Tasmania. Ivy went to dentists. We went to Empire in afternoon and the Pavillion at night. We came home by the 9.35pm. train with Daddy. Drove home in the moonlight. Had a really good time.

Sunday 18

Got up late. Miss Wilson, Mummy and Audrey went to Harvey's. A bee-keeper and Meyrick were here, L. Price and Dan also called. Merv cut his nose very badly. Miss Wilson and I took him to Farm, where he stayed all night. (Joe Green drowned.)

Monday 19

Washed in morning. Dan came in the afternoon and stayed for a while. Daddy and Merv went to Goodna in the morning. Big storm here about 7.30 pm. Ma came over at night. Got a ride over with Mr Honex. I stayed up until nearly 9 o'clock, reading. Merv's nose not hurting him much. There were 125 points of rain fallen in the storm.

Tuesday 20

Daddy and Merv went to Goodna this morning and brought young Tommy Parker home with them. He stayed until about 3.15 pm. Jim Rice also rode over and stayed for a while this evening. There was a storm about 5.30 pm. Miss Wilson and Audrey went over to the Farm and had afternoon tea there.

Wednesday 21

Nothing doing in morning except that Daddy and Merv went to Goodna. In the afternoon Miss Wilson and I went to Hebdens. We stayed until about 10 o'clock. Vera, May and Perce came across Ryan's paddock with us. Daddy and Merv drove to Ipswich. Jim and Mrs Rice and daughter came over for the afternoon and evening. Audrey went to the Farm in the morning.

Thursday 22

Mooched about all the morning. In the afternoon, Mat Kerwin came over to see Daddy. Miss Wilson went home today. Morgan and Lou Price came over about 4.30pm., played tennis till after dark, then after tea, played euchre until 10 o'clock. Mrs and Mr Hillier came over at night too. Mummy went over to Farm about 4 pm. Mrs MacDonald came up to see the kiddies.

Friday 23

Mummy, Audrey and I went to Brisbane and spent the day shopping. We went to the pictures for about an hour. Audrey went to the dentist. Roy Wilson came out. Morgan and Lou Price were over playing tennis, and we all played euchre at night until about 10 o'clock when they went home. Had a good day in Brisbane.

Saturday 24

Merv and Daddy went to Goodna in the morning and brought home case of fruit. In the afternoon, Maud and Nellie Yarrow, Ivy, Morgan and Meyrick came over and stayed the evening. We had tennis in the afternoon and music, dancing, and cards at night.

Sunday 25

Morgan and Meyrick came over in the afternoon to play tennis - some people from Ipswich also came for mangoes.

Monday 26

Holiday, being Foundation. Mummy and Ma took Audrey back to school. Daddy and Merv went to Goodna in cart. Roy Wilson rode Taffy down and got him shod. Garnet and Jessie Hillier came over. Maud and Nellie also came over for mangoes. I stayed over at the Farm with Ivy all day.

Tuesday 27

First State school day. Mummy and I washed. I sent notes to Vera and Miss Brennan with Merv, but Vera was away. Evelyn Hallett came for dinner and stayed until about 3.30pm. Had some music in the afternoon, and also a little at night.

Wednesday 28

Ironed nearly all day. Mummy trimmed my hat. In the afternoon I practised my music a bit. Morgan brought Dorritt, Larry, Secret and a few other horses from the creek. He was over for a game of cards at night. Roy was out looking for the horses in the morning, but did not find them. It was very hot all day. A hot wind was blowing until nearly dark. Fellow from Dinmore here for some mangoes.

Thursday 29

I went over to Hebden's for my music lesson about 10 o'clock. I had dinner there and came back with Vera. We led the chestnut as far as Harvey's and then Percy drove us from there. May, Eric and Mrs Hebden also drove over. Ivy and Keith came over for tennis. Two Rice's over for mangoes. Roy went to social in church. He and Perce were out shooting in the morning.

Friday 30

Mummy and I sewed nearly all day. Roy went over to Hebden's in the morning. In the afternoon, Uncle Lewis, Aunt Gwen and Nellie Jones were out here. Mr Roberts was out extracting honey all day. Roy went home. Morgan came over for tennis, and had cards at night. Some people came for mangoes.

Saturday 31

Came into town in morning. Had dinner at Wilson's and then went to Grammar School with Mummy and Roy. Coming back watched games of bowls and tennis. At night went to Martoo's pictures with Phyllis and Roy. Staying at Wilson's till Monday.

Sunday 1

Went to church in morning. Sunday school with Phil in the afternoon and then we both went up into the Park. Saw some people I know.

Monday 2

My first day at Grammar School. Came to school with Phyllis in the morning. Enjoyed a few lessons but did not like others. Missed my music lesson but practised in the afternoon after school. I am now going to bed. It is nearly nine o'clock. Like school fairly well. Ordered my books.

Tuesday 3

I got on better today. I had two practices of music. Was with Phil nearly all day. Am now going to bed. It is about nine o'clock. Liked my lessons better today. Also did more home lessons than last night. My books arrived.

Wednesday 4

Liked school still better today. Had my music lesson this afternoon and practised for an hour this morning. Wrote a letter to Mummy this morning also and posted it. Had a game of tennis this evening. Am now going to bed. Can't find any more "gas" so will shut up. 10 mo's later. I don't envy myself this first week.

Thursday 5

Liked school still better. Went to see Mummy in St. Andrew's Hospital this afternoon. Went through the Park. Lost one of Ivy's good handkerchiefs on the way back. Looking forward to going home. Went as far as St. Andrew's with Phyllis Wilson. Got message from Daddy in train.

70

Friday 6

Same programme as usual. Got telephone message from Daddy saying I could not go home today, to wait until tomorrow. Went to see Mummy this afternoon. She was getting on splendidly. Am all on my lonely-own tonight. I felt pretty vexed not going home.

Saturday 7

Came home from school. Ma, Daddy, and I went to station to see Auntie Audrey. Also saw Morgan. Dance in Hall at night. Band of Hope picnic. Dance in Goodna. Miss Wilson's birthday party. We all went to see Mummy in St. Andrew's. Getting on well. Saw Miss Brennan coming home.

Sunday 8

Miss Brennan came over. Ivy and I went home in afternoon. Daddy, Ivy and I drove to Goodna at night to get my dress fitted. Mr MacDonald came up.

Monday 9

Came back to school with Daddy in sulky this morning. Speaking to Mr Brennan for a while. Heard all about Miss Wilson's party from Phyllis. I went to see Mummy in the afternoon. She is getting on bonciferously. I stayed there a good while. Am now going to bed. Not allowed to have any supper tonight. My cold nearly better.

Tuesday 10

Same programme as usual. I did not go to see Mummy as I went for a walk with the other girls through the Park instead. I had my music lesson. Got on fairly well in school. Had a bit of a dance at night.

Wednesday 11

Just the same per usual. Had an English exam. Went down to St. Andrew's to see Mummy. Getting on real well. Is coming home with me on Friday. Had another bit of a dance at night. Going to bed now. Bit of a storm on, cats howling outside etc., to break the monotony of things. Looking forward to a good night's rest. P.S. Mosquitoes buzzing too.

Thursday 12
Same per every day. Went for a walk a good way past the East Ipswich Station this afternoon. I should have had book-keeping lessons, but could not as teacher did not turn up. Had another bit of a dance in "prep" room at night. Got up at six this morning to practise, so am going to bed tonight as soon as possible to make up for it. (Shut up)

Friday 13
School all day. Daddy called for me in the afternoon and drove Phyllis and me down town. Then I went up to St. Andrew's. Daddy came up soon after and drove Mummy and I home. Called at the Farm but did not go in. I got tea etc., as Mummy went straight to bed.

Saturday 14
Worked all day. Sold a good lot of mangoes in the morning while Daddy and Merv were away in Goodna. Daddy sold some in the afternoon. I did also. Mummy stayed in bed all day. Ivors and Audrey over in afternoon.

Sunday 15
Ma came over this morning. Mummy was up all the afternoon. Mrs Brennan over to see Mummy in evening. Ivy was over. Killed a green snake.

Monday 16
Came back to school again this morning. Daddy drove me to Goodna, and I came up to East Ipswich by train. Played, or pretended to play basket-ball this afternoon. Had history exam today and I got 38 per cent. Not too bad, for first time. Have a bad head ache now. It has been pretty bad all day.

Tuesday 17
Did not go for a walk today as I had to practise my music instead. Horrid! Had arithmetic examination today and I got, silly ass, 33 per cent by carelessness. Lots of girls got impots today, but I managed somehow to escape. Thinking I won't get any marks for drawing tomorrow as I have no book. Bit of shower this afternoon.

Wednesday 18

Had no exams today. Just going to have a basket ball game this afternoon, but the ball collapsed. Couldn't cry over it. Had an awful lot of lessons to learn for tomorrow. Missed my music lesson but managed to get my practice. Getting up early in morning so must hurry up and bump into bed. Looking forward to letter from home tomorrow. Also all the hardest exams.

Thursday 19

Had two most cruel exams today, science and drawing. Mine are most frightful. Terribly disappointed at not getting a letter this morning, but it arrived this afternoon. It has been raining nearly all day. Reading out to each other the "Australian Lassie" by Lilian Turner. Very nice so far. Looking forward to going home tomorrow. Percy Hebden died.

Friday 20

School as usual. Postponed my German exam until Monday. Came home by train this afternoon from E. Ipswich with Thelma, Hilda, and May McKee. Raining nearly all day. Drove home with Daddy from Goodna. Miss Conahan drove with us as far as her place. Met Mr Bevington in Goodna. Percy Hebden was buried in Toowong.

Saturday 21

Worked all day mostly. Mummy also did a great deal too much. Raining nearly all day. Ma and Keith came over in the evening. Some people came for mangoes. I stayed up pretty late reading. Wrote a letter to Aud.

Sunday 22

Raining a little all day. Meyrick came over in the afternoon. Ivy was also over. They played tennis for a while. Ivors came with Ivy. I wrote two letters.

Monday 23

Came back to school with Daddy this morning in sulky. Got a lovely bunch of roses coming in from Mrs Hensell, but sent them home to Mummy. Had my German exam, but did very badly I think. Didn't fall in love with school again much. Haven't got much time to write this as Miss Cadogan is coming to put the lights out.

Tuesday 24
Jolly old school again. Raining hard nearly all day. Had my music practise this afternoon, instead of going for a walk, and thus escaped an impot. Had a bit of a dance tonight, but only very little. Watched people on road to while away the time. Had tea early, and am now tumbling into bed.

Wednesday 25
School once more. Had a pretty good day. Didn't like my music lesson much. Only had about 8 minutes. Tonight Hilda and I short sheeted Thelma's bed. Wouldn't let Thelma in the door. Miss Hill saw us but only laughed. While I kindly went down to help Thelma Hilda pulled my bed on the floor, and Thelma pulled Hilda's. Great games. Looking forward to letters tomorrow.

Thursday 26
Got a letter from home. Disappointed in the morning about it, but it arrived in the afternoon. Miss White took me into her office for German. She was awfully nice. Phyllis brought Hilda and me some lovely flowers. Mummy was in town but didn't call to see me. Had my first book-keeping lesson today.

Friday 27
Came home today by train with Thelma. Waited in Goodna for Daddy and Audrey as they came up from Brisbane. Drove home with them. Received the results of my examination. Quite pleased with myself as I didn't expect it. Went to bed early. Entered for lecture on Monday night.

Saturday 28
Daddy, and Mummy went over to Hebden's in morning. In the afternoon, Mummy, Daddy and Audrey went to Welsh picnic and concert. Ivy and I went over to say "goodbye" to Hebden's. Then Merv and I stayed at the Farm all night. Merv went down for mail in morning.

Sunday 1
Audrey came over with Merv and me. This afternoon, Ivy and four kiddies came over. Lou Griffiths, Mr Pallister and Meyrick came over. Meyrick stayed for a while at night.

Monday 2

Came up to school by train this morning. Got on well. Had history exam and got 37 per cent. Gave parcel from home to Miss White to give to Phyllis. Went with others to Lecture on Wireless Telegraphy given by Mr. Fegan. Saw Miss Wilson, Mr and Roy Grimley there. Enjoyed it very much. A good many day girls also there.

Tuesday 3

Had arithmetic examination today and got 32 per cent by extraordinary superelificucious luck. Practised before walk this afternoon, therefore was able to go for it. We went through the Park, and Mr Terley (Turley) showed us through bush-house, hot-house, etc. We were talking to the birds also. Got invitation to go to Mrs Joe Rice's place.

Wednesday 4

Mummy and Daddy came up to see me this afternoon. Brought me up some persimmons and bananas. All the girls mates with me. Miss White called us all into the sitting-room tonight and gave us lectures on new rules for a time owing to certain circumstances. Looking forward to three exams. tomorrow (eh! What!). Book-keeping books have not arrived. Sprinkling rain nearly all day.

Thursday 5

Got no letters today as Mummy was in to see me yesterday. Mrs Brid Cribb was up here with ladies. Had three exams. today but do not know how I got on except it was pretty badly. Looking forward to going home tomorrow. A new girl from Thursday Island arrived today (Ruth George)

Friday 6

School as usual. Went home by train with the other girls. Daddy met me at station in Goodna. Drove Miss McKeon home, and then went round to Thomas' to get the paper. Went to bed fairly early, but stayed up talking to Mum for a while. Got word to tell Merv to be at cricket match in Goodna.

Saturday 7

Raining a little. Nothing startling happened. Mr Hebden came over with Dad and stayed all night (not forgetting Judy). Cricket match in Goodna, but Merv did not go. Mr and Mrs James' arrived on the Plains. Morgan and Meyrick came to play tennis and had cards at night.

Sunday 8

Morgan and Meyrick, Ivy and Keith were over in the afternoon. Mr Hebden and Judy went to Brisbane by the train leaving Goodna about 1 o'clock. Raining a little.

Monday 9

Raining pretty heavily all day. Came back to school this morning with Mummy, Ma and Topper (last but not least). It was very muddy all the way in, but not raining much just then. I brought some persimmons back with me, but they are not ripe yet. Practised this afternoon, and then yarned for about an hour in the boarders' sitting room.

Tuesday 10

Raining again nearly all day. Started my fancy work. Had a good school day. Practised this afternoon. No walk as it was too muddy and raining also. Third Form were not in school hall at preparation. Had dance. Got a splitting headache now. Didn't do much work, therefore, Mrs Mort. said she saw Uncle Dan.

Wednesday 11

At last the week is half over. Two of my persimmons were ripe. Jessie Coogan had one, (at least, I gave it to Jessie and all the kids had bite). Practised in prep. this afternoon. Did some fancy work. Played a set of tennis with Jessie Coogan, Laura Brazier and Ruth George. Ruth and I were beaten 6 games to 5. Am now going to bed, looking forward to all the Thursday lessons (I don't think).

Thursday 12

Practised early this morning. Got a letter this afternoon. Hilda and Thelma are having a fight, kicks, slaps resounding etc., so mistakes are excused. Got the giggles in study. Best laugh I have had for a long time. Had book-keeping lesson. I have been about 20 minutes writing this as I have been having rows about widths of foreheads, etc.

Friday 13

Audrey's birthday. Mummy and Ma called for me at school this evening. We went into town. Ma got her teeth done at dentist's while Mummy and I had an ice cream each. Did some more fancy work this morning. Syd. Griffiths died. We intended going to funeral, but missed it. Daddy brought Audrey home from Brisbane. Read out to Audrey for a good while tonight.

Saturday 14

Got up very late, and did a good deal of work. Ivy, Ivors, Keith, Audrey, and Thelma came over to Audrey's birthday tea. Morgan and Meyrick came over to play tennis. Ivy and Merv played also, but I didn't. They stayed at night when we played cards.

Sunday 15

Got up late. Did my lessons this morning. Daddy, Audrey and Merv went for a drive. Morgan, Meyrick, Lou Griffiths, and Ivy were over and played tennis in afternoon, and had music at night..

Monday 16

Came back to school by train this morning. Thought I had missed it but found I was 35 minutes too early. Mummy took Audrey back to school. We all drove down to Goodna together. Was umpire for basket ball this afternoon. Liked it much better than before. Got a bad head-ache. Got a rose from Phyllis. Had a good study tonight. Eau-de-cologne did head good.

Tuesday 17

Started drill today. At last the day is over. It seemed years. Didn't get on too well at lessons. Got 19% for arith. exam. Got into rows a bit at science. Hate it! No water today, so couldn't have a proper wash. Had a few games of tennis this afternoon. Miss White took study as Mrs Mort. had to go out for a time.

Wednesday 18

Got a letter from home today also enclosed in it one from Vera. Played basket-ball this afternoon for a good while. Can't rave about it. No water yesterday or today so couldn't have much of a wash. Have three exams. tomorrow, no preps. and book-keeping and basket-ball. I must say I am looking forward to it. Got on pretty fair with my lessons today.

Thursday 19

Had two examinations today, science and drawing. Heard that Mrs Mortimore had resigned. Played basket-ball for a while this afternoon. Had book-keeping instead of going for a walk. Been talking to Jessie Elsworthy at the window for the last half hour, scared Miss Lilley will come round, so better shut up. Am going to have another talk now.

Friday 20

Had three exams. today and only expecting one or two. Had no preps.. Came home from School today with Mummy and Ma. Went into town and had a cream puff. Saw Mrs Binney and children. Got home from town pretty late as Topper was tired. Saw several people I knew.

Saturday 21

Worked hard in morning. Got up late about 8.30 am. In the afternoon Daisy, Jessie Brennan and Ivy came over. We had music and tennis. They stayed till nearly dark. Mary B. came over with Jessie. I went to bed about 9 o'clock.

Sunday 22

Went to Creek for a picnic with Mummy and Merv. Ivors and Audrey over in morning. Dad went out also. Morgan, Meyrick, Ivy and Lou Griffiths over in afternoon.

Monday 23

Came back to school. Drove in with Mummy and Keith. Keith drove us in. Everything upside down today. I had to stay in and write out poetry five times because I did not know it for Miss Lilley. Practised this afternoon when Miss Cadogan hunted me there. Had a good talk to Jessie Elsworthy in her room where a couple of teachers nearly saw me.

Tuesday 24

Got on pretty well today. Had my music lesson this morning. Had two other preparations. Practised or pretended this afternoon while others went for a walk. From 3.45 pm to 4.45 pm Thelma, Miriam and I sewed in the arbour. Got English exam. tomorrow, so not feeling too well altogether.

Wednesday 25

Got on alright. Raining hard nearly all day. Had no drill or games this afternoon. Had English exam. for hour lesson. This afternoon was summoned before the court of Lilley (Miss Lilley's room) where I received such a lecture on my most fearful writing. I enjoyed it more than I have done anything for a long time. Am at my wit's ends I have so much to do for tomorrow. O shut up.

Thursday 26

Had book-keeping again as usual. Got two home letters. The trustees came to visit the school this afternoon. Eric Scott only one I knew that I saw. Got English exam. results. Managed to get 39% but dreadful writing (all book). A lot of girls got into a scrape for not going for a walk. Looking forward to tomorrow.

Friday 27

Day went past very quickly. Had last lesson out in garden. Went down town with Phyllis, left my basket in the sulky and did some shopping. Drove home in the dark with Daddy. Had our tea as we came - gingerbeer, biscuits, fairy cakes and bananas. It was a most spliferous drive.

Saturday 28

Got up very late. Worked nearly all the morning. Ironed all the afternoon. It was raining pretty heavily nearly all day so couldn't get my clothes dry. Stayed up pretty late at night. Wasn't too well. Finished reading "A Big Horse to Ride".

Sunday 29

Stayed in bed until dinner time. Mummy and I not too well. Read "On a Bush Track" - glorious. Ivy was over this afternoon, also Mr Ben Josey. Am now to bed at 9 o'clock.

Monday 30

Came back to school per usual with Mummy in sulky. Received a braille letter from Audrey - caused great sensation. Had two big slices of beautiful cake. Am writing this in the dark as lights are supposed to be out. Just as Miss Cadogan came in I found my bed was short-sheeted. Nearly fell in. Some more girls in our class.

Tuesday 31

Got on all right until this afternoon when nearly all the school had to stay in for half an hour and do sums. Had to write an essay on "Valour" for tomorrow. Was umpire for basket-ball this afternoon. I wrote to Mummy and Vera this morning. Am rowing with Thelma all the time I'm writing.

Wednesday 1

Got through today somehow. Had a bad head-ache this afternoon and had my last "Aspirin". Had to play basket-ball twice so that did not improve it in the least. Miss Hill on duty tonight so have to hurry up and get into bed. Got tons of work for tomorrow and have done a good deal of it. Pretty hot today. The lists for travelling came out and I was marked "Private".

Thursday 2

Week is nearly over. Mummy, Keith and Ma came up to see me. Keith brought me a box of chocolates. All finished now. This time next week I will be at home. Had last book-keeping this time. Mr Jones was awfully nice. Got tons of German for tomorrow. Must say, am looking forward to it as not finished.

Friday 3

Came home by train with Ruby from school. Mummy drove us home from Goodna. Got flowers from Thelma in the train. The last Friday to spend at school before Easter. It is lovely.

Saturday 4

Had breakfast in bed. Just fooled around all the morning. In the afternoon played tennis with Merv, Morgan, Meyrick and Ivy. Audrey, Ivors, Thelma were over also. Played cards at night.

Sunday 5

Got up late. Ruby and I went to creek and got ferns this morning. Meyrick was over to play tennis. Ivy and Merv went over to Juillerat's for a ride.

Monday 6

Drove back to school with Mummy and Ruby this morning. Got some chocolates on the way in. Mummy forgot to take Merv's so it is eaten now. Managed to get through school somehow. Had a bit of a head-ache, but cheered up as it is last Monday at school.

Tuesday 7
My eye is nearly all right today. Still a bit swollen. German and Latin marks read out but no more. Most beautiful sunset I have ever seen this afternoon. Teacher's meeting this afternoon. Mrs Mortimores's last day on duty. Is to be presented with a silver ink stand tomorrow.

Wednesday 8
Lot of girls went home today. Great excitement. Can hardly wait for tomorrow to come. Ruby not feeling too good tonight as has to stay all holidays. I have packed nearly all my clothes in my basket. Had a most glorious English hour lesson this afternoon. Best we ever had. Had a bit of a dance tonight.

Thursday 9
Came home from school with Mummy. Just as we finished tea, Daddy, Audrey and Miss Shepherd arrived to stay till Tuesday. In the afternoon we had 5 mins off each lesson. Had an early time-table, and therefore got out of school at about twenty to three. So therefore got home early.

Friday 10
Went out to the Creek with Morgan (driving), Merv, Ivy, Daisy and Maud. Went out about 10 o'clock. About 30 (-1) visitors at the Creek. Went up on Mount Calvary. Had a lovely day. Drove home after sun-set. Most beautiful drive any of us have ever had.

Saturday 11
Nurse Alton was out all day. She went for a ride with Daddy to lemon tree at creek in the afternoon. Audrey and I read under a mango tree. Zilpha Hillier, Ivy Rix and Morgan Jones over here this afternoon. Audrey staying at Farm all night tonight.

Sunday 12
Audrey came home from Farm with Merv. Ivy came over in afternoon and we (Ivy, Merv, Audrey and I) went for a walk round lane etc..

Monday 13

Uncle Jim over early in morning. About 11 o'clock, Mr and Mrs Lewis and party came out in two vehicles for a picnic here. They had a good time. In the afternoon we had music for a good while. Mrs Reece sang as she has a glorious contralto voice. Mrs Lewis, Dillis, and Audrey also contributed towards the programme.

Tuesday 14

Audrey and Miss Shepherd went back to school. I went over to dressmaking class with Mummy and Ivy. Read all day at the back of billiard room. Had a talk to all the girls. Tried to do a line, but didn't succeed. Had a look at the billiard room. Went up to Jones' and Rice's. Saw Ham's baby and asked how Jim was.

Wednesday 15

Washing day. I didn't do much. Just fooled around all day until at night I ironed and played marbles with Merv. Daddy went to Brisbane at night to a meeting. Lou Griffiths came over at night and stayed till a little after twelve o'clock. I practised for a good while in the evening.

Thursday 16

Mummy, Ma and I went down to Brisbane by the 10 o'clock train. We did a bit of shopping and then went to the Art Gallery where we stayed for over an hour. After dinner we went to the Pictures and after doing a little more shopping we came home. Mr Roberts had sulky waiting at station, so we came straight home.

Friday 17

Got up about 9 o'clock. Mummy was sewing all day. I was just fooling around. Jim Rice came over in the afternoon and I got afternoon tea for him and Mummy. I got a letter from Ruby Rayner and a birthday card from Mr Hebden. Went to bed pretty early. Looking forward to banquet tomorrow night.

Saturday 18

Went over as far as the Farm with Daddy and Merv. Came straight back and brought Ivors with me. At night, we all went over to Hebden's presentation affair and had a rattling good time. Nearly everyone enjoyed it. Lel H. stayed for dance.

Sunday 19

Got up about 10 o'clock. Did some lessons etc.. Morgan, Meyrick, Ma, Mr MacDonald, Audrey and Thelma were over this afternoon. Expecting Lou G. and Lel H., but never turned up.

Monday 20

Came back to school once more. Stayed at farm for a while. Before I came to school, Merv and Neb caught a hare. A lot of new girls came. The new teacher, Miss Carmody from Rockhampton took us for hour-lesson geography. Last, but not by any means least, I celebrated? my birthday.

Tuesday 21

Had new teacher again today. Beautiful sunset this afternoon. Had my music lesson this morning. Told Miss Cadogan I hadn't practised. She said she didn't expect me to. Really nice of her. Played tennis in the hour-prep and as a matter of course I won. Practised this afternoon.

Wednesday 22

Just jumbled through today somehow. Had some cocoanut ice to sweeten it up however. Had a lovely English lesson. Had arith. lesson by new teacher. Dodged taking exercise this afternoon. Sat down near the swings with Jessie Coogan and Thelma Graham. Nearly standing on my head so much in a whirlwind with lessons for tomorrow. Something cruel!

Thursday 23

Hilda saw someone walking in their sleep near our room, striking matches, so am feeling pretty shaky. Had a very hard day but at last it is over. Played basket-ball for about three-quarters of an hour. Had another book-keeping lesson also a German one, alas! Had half science lesson in garden. Got a letter from home.

Friday 24

At last the end of the week came. Had a pretty hard day but scrambled through somehow. Came home in sulky with Mummy and Topper (eh)? Nothing exciting happened. There was a meeting at school after I left about a student Christian Society or something like that. A Miss Hamilton conducted the meeting. .

Saturday 25
Dad and Merv left home before seven am and spent the day in Brisbane. Came home by last train. Mummy and I went over to the Farm for tea and came home in the dark. Four kids over in morning. Daddy bought me a tennis racquet.

Sunday 26
Got up late and had medicine! D.-Madness! Don't be shocked, you who are inquisitive enough to read, but I did my lessons and played tennis this afternoon.

Monday 27
Came back to school this morning with Mummy in sulky. Had the most cruel German lesson ever I had. Went out with Miss Hill and seven other girls tonight to see "The Arcadians". It was lovely. Liked Jack Meadows, Bobbie, Sombra and Eileen Cavanagh the best. Miss White saw us down there, but did not go in or come home with us. (History exam).

Tuesday 28
Had my music lesson in the hour prep., therefore couldn't play tennis. Played tennis this afternoon with Jessie Coogan, Margaret Gillies and Miriam Luck. Had a pretty good time with lessons. Got a pretty bad cold. Thelma acting the goat, so am all muddled. Wrote a letter home today.

Wednesday 29
Scraped through the day somehow. This week is going very slowly. Got two letters today, one from Vera and one from Mummy. Played tennis this afternoon for a while. The firsts as 'present girls' played 'old girls' this afternoon and won by 51 points. Had nice English hour-lesson. Practised for three-quarters of an hour this afternoon in prep. of course.

Thursday 30
Most awful day but crawled through somehow. Terrible lessons and didn't feel too well all day. Had no book-keeping lesson, as teacher, Mr Jones did not turn up. Played tennis this afternoon. There was a meeting at dinner-time about Christian Students' Association but so far have not joined.

Friday 1
Should have had gymnastics but got excused for the day. Mummy called for me, and we went into town. Came home about dark. Audrey & Leila came home from Brisbane with Daddy. Were home when we got there. Phyllis got offended at something or other.

Saturday 2
Ivors' birthday. Got up late. Went over to Farm in the afternoon with Leila & Audrey to Ivors' afternoon tea. Merv went to dentists. All came home from Farm about dark & got scared by some cows. At least, I was, as I was only one not riding.

Sunday 3
Lew Griffiths & Jim Rice were over in afternoon & had a game of tennis. I had a bad cold.

Monday 4
Miss Lilley was in a ——— temper. Came back to school again with Mummy, Merv & Audrey & Topper. Had no exams. Except geography which made up for about five. Most awful. Played tennis this afternoon with Thelma & Muriel Collins. Had a head-ache. Finished aspirins.

Tuesday 5
Had arithmetic exam. this morning - Results not out yet. Had a pretty nice music lesson. Posted a letter for Miss White in Latin. Read a lot of "The Virginian". Found out all sorts of explanations why Phyllis was out of sorts. Don't know what to put, so will ring off.

Wednesday 6
Had English exam. Haven't got over the effects yet. Looking forward to two exams tomorrow. Got a letter from home. Asked Chrissie Bourke about going out there. Just been told I don't eat enough, so going to have a mouth all over my face now. Have been arguing etc., so better shut up!

Thursday 7

Had a cruel day, German lesson & two exams - science & drawing. Had book-keeping this afternoon. Had a lovely study tonight. Settled about going out to Bourke's. Played tennis this afternoon with Jessie Coogan, Muriel Collins, & Evelyn Horton. Can't realise today is over. Looking forward to German exam.

Friday 8

Had first gymnastics today. Didn't go home, but went to Bourke's with Chrissie. Got there pretty late as was late leaving gymnastics. Played corner nearly all night. Was sitting on the verandah for a good while with Chrissie, Allan & Mr Bourke. Are a real nice family & I enjoyed the evening alright.

Saturday 9

Read for 6 hours. Raining, - rather pouring - all day. Went down town with Chrissie to meet Mummy, & to my surprise found her there. Met Miss Wilson & was talking to her for a good while. Came home & I went straight to bed. Finished "The Virginian".

Sunday 10

Did my lessons today. Aunt Eve & Uncle Jim rode over in the afternoon. I was sick & had no tea, but I felt much better afterwards when I took soda or something.

Monday 11

Came back to school by train this morning. Daddy drove me to Goodna with Larry. Came up by train with Hilda and Thelma. Had a good time. Had a fair day. Got results of English exam. Got 45%. Can't get over it. Also got German results. Got 12%.

Tuesday 12

Pretty good day. Bridge party on tonight. Going down to have a look but changed my mind as might be copped & have enough to do without impots.. Had a pretty awful music-lesson. Rather nice science lesson. Only I was asked all the questions. The bridge party is rankling in my mind. It is disgusting us not having anything.

Wednesday 13
Got through hour-lesson somehow. Supposed to play tennis this afternoon but only sat on side of court & watched. Had a pretty bad headache this afternoon but nearly all right now. Got tons, cwts. & tons more of lessons for tomorrow, so am feeling very happy. Thelma just told us her essay. Never laughed so much for a long time. Must shut up, as must learn my dialogue.

Thursday 14
Just got through today in a fashion. Had a most cruel German lesson & a nice book-keeping lesson this afternoon. Played tennis this afternoon with Alice Andrews, Jessie Coogan, & Muriel Collins. Had chocolate pudding for dinner. No more news so will shut up now (with love from Qu) sorry. - most humbly apologise.

Friday 15
Came home with Mummy & Merv in sulky with Topper. Went into town and shopped till dark. Came home in the dark. Miss Shepherd & Miss Taylor were there when we arrived. Went to bed about 10 o'clock. Liked gymnastics much better today. Raining a little.

Saturday 16
Raining nearly all day. I practised in the morning while all the rest but Daddy were away. At night all the actors & actresses of dialogue came over & we had a rehearsal. Had great fun - am sore from laughing.

Sunday 17
Raining this afternoon. Went down to the Creek & had dinner there. We also gathered maiden-hair, etc.. Getting packed up for school.

Monday 18
Drove down to Goodna with Merv, Miss Shepherd & Miss Taylor. Sat on Miss Shepherd's knee. Daddy also went to Brisbane & rode down to Goodna. I came up by train with other Grammar girls. Had a terrible history exam. Pretty nice German & English lessons.

Tuesday 19
Fair day. Pretty good music lesson. Got results of history exam - 40. Pretty nice science lesson. Also had pretty good arithmetic exam this morning. Results not out yet. Played tennis this afternoon with Gladys C. & Doris W. Another bridge party tonight. Had a bit of a squiz at it. Style.

Wednesday 20
Fairly good day, but nearly mad with lessons for tomorrow. Had English exam. today. Fair exam. Hilda & I were shown by Miss Woods this morning how to walk down stairs. Played tennis with Thelma T., Olive B., & Ruth G.. Just found my dialogue today so must learn it now. Going to clean goloshes now so must shut up.

Thursday 21
Worst day I've had this term. Had three exams. - science, geography, & drawing. Two results, got 43 for geography & 25 for drawing. Didn't get a letter from home so don't know what to think. Raining nearly all day. Looking forward to German exam. tomorrow.

Friday 22
Had a pretty fair day. Got out from gymnastics early. Mummy & Merv called for me. Stayed in town & shopped until about half-past six. Came home & called at a few places about the concert on the way. Got home pretty late & Dad & Audrey had tea ready.

Saturday 23
Got up late. Practised a bit & fooled around. Mummy finished my new dress. At night most of the dialogue people came over to practise & we had a good time. Ivy stayed over all night. Morgan also stayed for the night.

Sunday 24
Audrey & I had breakfast in bed. Ivy went home early. Morgan went home before dinner. Meyrick over at night. A & I went to Farm.

Monday 25

Came back to school by train. Daddy drove Audrey & me down to Goodna while Ivy rode. She took Audrey to Brisbane. Miss White let us see the cadet's procession in prep. Tonight. We were so loyal - doing patriotic songs, etc., with Mrs. G. as leader. Pretty sick.

Tuesday 26

Had a really nice music lesson. Also a nice science lesson - not a bad day altogether. Wrote a letter home about the show. Had a bit of a headache but got alright after a bit. Another bridge party tonight. 'Tisnt a bit fair.

Wednesday 27

Had a fair day. Had a pretty good English lesson. Played tennis match with R. George. Beat Kathleen Harsant & Muriel Collins with one game but was beaten by Eileen Foote & Dorothy Creaser in the next. Cleaned my shoes so the black won't come off my hands. Had a short study tonight as have two lessons less tomorrow.

Thursday 28

Had half holiday & went to the Show with Mummy, Daddy & Merv. Had a really good afternoon. Went to Wilson's for tea. Came back & stayed until about half past nine. Mummy & Daddy drove me back & then went on home. Merv stayed at Pickering's all night as he has to go to the dentist's tomorrow. (Made a resolution?)!!

Friday 29

Came home with Mummy in sulky. Met Merv in town with the Pickerings. Drove home pretty early. I stayed at the Farm all night & Mummy & Merv went on home. Ivy & I slept together in her single bed. Had a great time.

Saturday 30

Came home with Audrey B. about half-past ten, who stayed until afternoon when Ivors & Thelma came over for her. Only half of the dialogue people came for rehearsal. Went through it though. Also played "euchre". Ivy went home this morning. Meyrick came over to play tennis. Mrs Smith, Violet & Myrtle were out for the afternoon.

Monday 1
Pretty good day. Had history exam. but not expecting much
for results. Drove in to school this morning with Mummy &
Thelma. Thelma had to go to the dentist's. All of us were kept
in by Miss Hill (pig!!!) for laughing at a great joke.

Tuesday 2
Fair day. Another bridge party tonight. Looking forward to
holiday tomorrow. Had a pretty good music lesson this
afternoon & very fair other lessons. Thelma went home this
afternoon so Hilda & I are all alone in our glory tonight.
Just cleaned shoes etc., so am pretty black.

Wednesday 3
A Holiday. Something unusual. Read all the morning &
played tennis for half-an-hour. Iced vovos for lunch. Read
afternoon until about half-past three. Then went with other
girls, in charge of Sixth form, to the Park where we had
afternoon tea as a Picnic. Then went & watched the Town
Club playing tennis. Came home, had tea & read nearly all
the evening. Had a little dancing & music.

Thursday 4
Had a lovely German lesson - about the best since Easter & a
fair science lesson. Had English exam. but hadn't half
finished when the bell rang. Played tennis for half-an-hour
this afternoon with Alice Andrews, Evelyn Horton, & Jessie
Coogan. Had a fair book-keeping lesson & a fair headache,
as well. Thelma came back this morning.

Friday 5
Came home in sulky with Mummy & Merv. Went to Griffith' to
tea. Then went to Hall where we had a grand rehearsal.
Stayed until about 10 o'clock. Then drove home with
Mummy & Ivy while Merv. rode. Raining fairly heavily all
day, but cleared up a bit at night. Got new shoes.

Saturday 6
(in her mother's handwriting: "No Concert")
Worked hard all day. Rained pretty good deal in morning
but of course it must rain heavily about four o'clock until
about 9. Daddy went to Goodna to meet Hebdens' but they
didn't arrive.

Sunday 7
(got bet of icecream)
Stayed in bed until dinner-time. Went over to Farm with Mummy. Mrs Josey was there. Morgan was over in afternoon. Played tennis, & stayed for the evening.

Monday 8
Drove into school this morning with Mummy & Thelma. Had a pretty good day. Had awful geography exam.. Fair English lesson. Miss Woods on duty. Also bridge party is on tonight instead of tomorrow night. Got no lessons done for tomorrow.

Tuesday 9
Pretty good day. Had a lovely music-lesson, short and sweet. Miss Lilley went away this afternoon so hoping she won't be here tomorrow. Had a headache when I woke but it soon wore off when I took half an aspirin. Practised in the dark this evening and had some fun.

Wednesday 10
Nice day. Had a glorious English lesson, but exam. not out yet. Geography exam. however came out. I got 35%. Alice Andrews beat me for 2nd time this year. Lot of girls went to St. Pauls' thing-me-bob. Teachers went to Hospital Ball. Miss Carmody was on duty tonight for first time. Miss White should have taken study, but didn't. However she is on duty now, so must hurry to get to bed!

Thursday 11
Thought I was in for an awful day but it wasn't so bad. Had two exams - science & drawing. They are our last two exams, this time. Had a fair book-keeping lesson. Miss Lilley on duty, so must hurry up. Packing up to go home, too. Lovely. Looking forward to concert. Got a letter from home.

Friday 12
Pretty nice weather today. Went home in trap with Mummy. Went to Hall for the rehearsal. L.L. did not turn up so we were all wild and couldn't practise properly. Came home very tired at night. Saw Miss Wilson in town who said she was coming out on Saturday night. Saw Ted P. & R.G., & a few more!!!

Saturday 13
Miss Hebden came up. Sun shone in morning. Got darker in afternoon until at night it just simply poured. There were 130 points at our place (of rain). We had a bonciferous dance, in spite of it, however. Mr Murdo Scotch singer, & Miss Jones, & a few others were out & waited in Hall till morning.

Sunday 14
Pretty fine day. Mummy drove Miss Hebden back to train, called for me at Farm & drove home together. Morgan over while we were away, & Mr Hillier there when we got home.

Monday 15
Came back to school by train. Drove as far as Goodna with Larry. Gave Miss Connahun a drive. Raining nearly all day. Had nice lessons. Had prep. instead of singing this afternoon as I had a cold. Thought I had to work sums for "Beauty" but she repented & let us do prep. instead. Very tired now.

Tuesday 16
Had a nice day & a nice music-lesson. Told Miss C. I hadn't practised in week-end, so she never gave me much. Raining nearly all day. No walk. I practised at 3.45pm instead of 4.45pm. No bridge party tonight. It is very cold just now so must get into bed quickly & we have been fooling.

Wednesday 17
Coldest day we have had this winter. Miss Lilley felt it so badly that she let us go early from drill. Had a really nice English lesson. No rain today for a wonder, but oh! such an icy wind. It was awful. My cold not too bad. This week going very quickly. Miss Woods on duty & nearly forgot to put our lights out. So in consequence we had a good time. Miss Hill came in to stop our noise.

Thursday 18
Had a fairly nice day. Got a post-card from home with an awful lot of news in it. Took me all day to read it (I don't think). Played tennis for half-an-hour this afternoon in the cold. A little rainified today, but not quite so cold as yesterday. Getting packed up for going home tomorrow.

Friday 19
Drove home with Mummy in sulky. She didn't call for me until about half-past four. Had given up hopes of ever going home. Never went back into town so got home early in consequence. Nothing exciting happened. Had pretty good lessons. Had a gymnastic lesson. Liked it a bit better than usual.

Saturday 20
Went to Brisbane by the 10 train. Saw Roy W. on the way down. Went out to see Audrey with Ivy. Came back into town, met Daddy, & all went to "The Forty Thieves" - most glorious. Came home by 20min. to 5 train. Came home with Mrs. Gibson in train.

Sunday 21
Rode up to the "Bees" in morning with Merv & Ivy. In afternoon, games, Mr Pallister, Morgan & Meyrick J., Ivors & Audrey, were over. Had a few sets of tennis.

Monday 22
Nice day. Miss Lilley got into a "rat" at English. Miss Hill copped us about a quarter past nine at night with our beds on the floor. Went off the handle. Had a nice singing-lesson, most of the time watching some men trying to capture a lunatic, thief or something across the road.

Tuesday 23
Had a nice day. Pretty bad music-lesson. The painters started scraping, and going on today, so will have the school painted soon. Week going very quickly. Played tennis with Chrissie B., Edna H., & Alice A. this afternoon. Thelma not here tonight as went to Foote's for the night.

Wednesday 24
Had a lovely English lesson. Read all the time. Finished the "Princess". Packed most of my books away this afternoon & also my basket. Supposed to play in monthly matches but it rained, so couldn't. School started getting painted today. Had fights with Thelma this afternoon, while packing. Got lots of lessons for tomorrow & going to be dressed by six!! (I wonder)!!!!

Thursday 25

Had a nice day. Raining heavily nearly all day. A scholarship girl arrived today to go in tomorrow. Went to Boys' Grammar Concert in all the slosh-bosh and mud at night. Miss White in an awful rats. Said we were all lunatics except about six - hope I'm one of these. (insert: which?) Concert was very nice. "Little Lord Fauntleroy" is a darling. Got home about 11 o'clock, I think.

Friday 26

Bonser day. Early timetable. Got out of school at something to three. Had gymnastics. Daddy drove in for me with Ma's sulky & Larry. Very muddy roads. Scholarships at school for first day of their examination. Two of them had dinner with us. Great excitement as most of the kids went. Mummy & Myfanwy went to Audrey's concert & bring her home. Stayed at farm all night.

Saturday 27

Came over from Farm about nine o'clock on the muddy roads. Daddy went to Goodna & Merv went to Ipswich with Mr Fox to get his teeth attended to. Ivors & Thelma came over in the afternoon. Raining a little now & then.

Sunday 28

Ivy, Keith, Morgan & Meyrick came over. We played tennis all the afternoon & at night had music. Morgan & I lost our "Harry Lauder" set of tennis 6-4.

Monday 29

First real Midwinter holiday. Two nurses from St. Andrew's came out - Nurse Gilfort? & Nurse Ibert. Plenty of life in them. In the afternoon Ma came over & we had lots of music. Mummy drove nurses back. Myfanwy & Audrey went home with Ma. Myfanwy came back with Mummy & Audrey stayed all night.

Tuesday 30

Washing day. I washed two sulkies, helped wash, & chipped the tennis-court. Never worked so hard for a long time. Ivy came over in morning & had a game of tennis. Daddy went to Brisbane & brought Dora back with him. Audrey came home at night. Merv went to Goodna in morning and farm in the afternoon. home at night. Merv went to Goodna in morning and farm in the afternoon.home at night. Merv went to Goodna in morning and farm in the afternoon.

Wednesday 1

Audrey & I took Myfanwy & Vera for a walk (a run!) to the creek in the morning. In the afternoon all the rest of us with Ivy, Ivors, Audrey, Thelma & Keith went up to the "Bees" for a picnic. Had afternoon tea there, went for a walk to the top of the hill & had a look all round. Came home jolly tired. Eating "flucorchas" (?) nearly all day.

Thursday 2

Went for butter to Harvey's in the morning with Vera. Waited for cream-man at the "Bees". In the afternoon, Vera & I walked, and Mummy, Myfanwy & Audrey drove, over to Rices'. Had afternoon tea there & Vera & I walked home in the moonlight. The others drove to Halletts'. Nearly going to a social in Goodna at night, but didn't.

Friday 3

Vera & I ate flauquartius under the tree all the morning. In the afternoon we went up to the "Bees" to get pepperinas for decorations. At night, Mummy, Ivy & I went to rehearsal. Everybody turned up & had a good time. Had some music & dancing.

Saturday 4

Vera & I went over to James' in the morning. At night went over to concert - was a great success. The dialogue very good. Vera & May came home in motor, & Roy Wilson drove home with Mummy.

Sunday 5

Got up early. In the afternoon we played tennis. Raining a little. Vera & May went home. Morgan, Meyrick, Ivy & Mat. Kerwin here.

Monday 6

First state school day. Got up about 10 o'clock. Keith started school. Joe Gardner came over in evening to see Daddy. All except Daddy went over to the Band of Hope tonight. Fairly good. Audrey recited "What I Live For". Arranged to get our photos taken in dialogue.

Tuesday 7
Audrey, Mummy & I went to Ipswich about 12 o'clock &
returned about 7 o'clock. Roy stayed at Farm all day.
Daddy went to Brisbane. Pictures in Hall at night, but never
went. Got silk to make me a new dress.

Wednesday 8
Washing day. I didn't do much. At night, Mummy, Merv and
I drove Topper and Ivy & Roy rode Secret and Taffy, to
Paget's Pictures in the Hall. They were really good. "East
Lynne" was star piece, also "Arachne & Minerva" etc. Some
competitions & music also. Very cold driving home but all
the same very nice as it was moon-light. Got the rainbow
cake for Audrey. Audrey stayed at "Farm" all night.

Thursday 9
Went over to "Farm" for Audrey in the morning. At night
went over to James' & had music, etc.. Lovely moonlight
coming home. Daddy put pane of glass in the kitchen window. Very windy day - the third one. Did nothing else, so
will have to shut off steam. Morgan over in afternoon &
played tennis.

Friday 10
Audrey & I got up late. I washed some floors. Ivy over in
morning. Daddy went to Brisbane & brought home Cissy
Saunders with him. Mummy made Audrey a new dress.
Audrey knitted nearly all day. I arranged the postcards in
the albums, & also read most of "Ivanhoe" - bonzer.

Saturday 11
Audrey & Cissy went for a drive with Daddy in the morning. Audrey stopped at "Farm" & Cissy & Dad went on to
Goodna. Played tennis with Roy in the afternoon. Audrey
gave us a musical evening. Getting Audrey's clothes
ready for school.

Sunday 12
Went for a picnic to the hill near Gardner's. Morgan &
Meyrick over to play tennis & stayed the evening. I read
out to Audrey & Cissy.

Monday 13

Went to Brisbane with Mummy, Ma, Roy, Audrey & Cissy Saunders. Went out to Institution, then by Ips. Rd. tram to town, went to Art Gallery, Aunt Bess', had dinner, went to Museum which was closed, so came back & had a walk all round Wickham Terrace. Ma was shopping all day. Had a really good day.

Tuesday 14

Roy & I went over to dress-making class with Mummy & Ivy. Ivy rode & we drove. Roy & I stayed outside in the sun all day, & read and talked. Called at Holland's coming home & thus came home by the school. Had a bit of a dance in the afternoon in the Hall. Played "bobs" at night.

Wednesday 15

Washing day. I got up late, washed up then went down & helped Mummy to wash. Dad drove to Goodna & met Roy Grimley. Arrived about dinnertime. Roy W., Roy G., & I played "bobs" nearly all the afternoon and evening. Had some music at night as well - piano, violin & singing. Mummy wrote notes asking girls to come over on Friday.

Thursday 16

Mummy & Ma went to Brisbane & brought the Waghorns home. I went over to Farm & stayed with Ivy & Edna all day. Daddy went to Goodna in morning. All went over to Post Office meeting at night, but Mummy & I stayed with Mrs. James as no other ladies came to the meeting. Arrived home about 10.45pm.

Friday 17

Got up late. Roy W. went to Goodna to get Taffy shod & brought home some chocolates. Expecting girls, but they didn't come. Played tennis in the afternoon, & "bobs" as well. Mummy & I ironed. I made a rosette. Had bobs, cards, music & dancing at night - a kind of a party.

Saturday 18

Roy Grimley went home in the morning - drove with Daddy to Goodna. Roy Wilson went home about dinner-time - walked with Merv. We went & got our physogues taken. At night went to Rice's "Coin Evening", had a day of it alto-gether. Ivy had a bad headache.

Sunday 19
Got up late. Went over to the Farm. Ivy's head still aching. Morgan & Meyrick & Mat Kerwin over, who played tennis in afternoon & bobs at night. Getting packed for school.

Monday 20
First schoolday after Midwinter Holidays. Miss Lilley in a good bit of a temper. Raining heavily in the morning. Cleared up a bit in the afternoon. Intended driving in this morning, but had to come by train as it was wet. Got different room mates tonight, & Thelma & Hilda are shifted out for a night or so.

Tuesday 21
Had a nice day - it passed very quickly. Had a lovely music-lesson. Had a long, long walk this afternoon. I went, as I did not practise the same time as last term. Got on really well in science. We are all back in our own rooms again now, so much more comfortable.

Wednesday 22
Week passing awfully quickly. Had bonser English lesson, Miss Lilley did nothing but get red & tear about the whole lesson. Played tennis this afternoon. Should have played croquet but got out of it. This afternoon had a prep. First time I have had this prep. Phyllis brought some violets - gave me a few. Miss Woods told Phyllis & me that we were to arrange the tennis matches for the ladder in our form - Awful Humbug. Got letter & photo from home.

Thursday 23
Had a pretty bad German lesson. Not bad English lesson. First book-keeping lesson this term. Two new kids started. Got another letter from home this morning. Sent photo home with Phyllis. Worst day over, so am feeling very thankful - looking forward to going home. Feeling very sleepy.

Friday 24

Not extra good German Lesson. Got a lovely bunch of roses from Roy. Came home by train & brought Winnie Harrison home with me. Audrey & Miss Shepherd also came home. The Premier, Mr Blair, etc. came out to the Plains to hold a meeting. Mr Waghorn at Farm - came yesterday. Went to bed about nine o'clock, I think.

Saturday 25

Winnie & Audrey drove to Goodna with Daddy in the morning. In afternoon, the James' were over & we played tennis. Mr Appleton came over & took photos at the Farm. Miss Shepherd showed us some bonser photos.

Sunday 26

Got up late. Went for picnic. Mr Humphreys, Mr Appleton, Mr & Mrs Tommy Waghorn, Mr Josey & Ivy were over. I went for a ride. Ivy, Merv, & Miss Shepherd rode to Juillerat's.

Monday 27

Drove back to school with Mummy & Winnie. Took Mummy's purse with me, and she had to come back for it. New time-table today - pretty hard one, but managed to scrape through somehow. Miss Hill has told us to put out our light so must hurry up. Found I was to be in the Work Stall at the Bazaar - horrid.

Tuesday 28

Got on real well. Had a pretty fair music-lesson, considering all things. Had nice lessons. Umpired for some tennis matches, & played one this afternoon. I won, 21-8 from Evelyn Horton. On top of it, went for a walk right down to the River & back. 'Twas very nice. Had glorious lecture on "India" by Miss Russell, Missionary.   Got Joey.

Wednesday 29

Practised at 6.30 a.m. Had a lovely English-lesson. This afternoon played in the monthly matches & lost of course. Played 3 sets altogether. Got tons of work for tomorrow, & to cap it all, I have to practice at 6 am. Had a fair music-lesson this morning. Miss Cadogan roused a bit. Week not passing so quickly as it might.   Rats.

Thursday 30
A most dreadful - Cruel, Cruel, cruel English Exam. 4 questions & I had not quite finished 2, & those are dreadful. Got a letter from home today. Looking forward eagerly to tomorrow. Miss Lilley not in an extra good mood. Got no more news. Think there's a fire in town so going to have a look with Thelma. Played tennis this afternoon.

Friday 31
Had a really nice day. Mummy drove in for me about half-past four. We went into town & did some shopping. Met Mrs & Gracie Lingard. Called round at Wilson's & brought Miss Wilson home with us. Had our tea at Farm. Also had some music. Daddy went to Brisbane & came home by last train.

Saturday 1
(Merv's first attempt at a dialogue). Did nothing particular. Practised in the morning. In the afternoon got my war-paint on. At night went to Band of Hope & Mrs Gorman's social. Mr & Tom Waghorn were over in the afternoon & stayed for tea. Had fair day.

Sunday 2
Got up about 9 o'clock. Did my lessons in morning. In the afternoon walked with Mummy & Miss Wilson to James' then to Picnic on the Flat. Called at Farm coming home. Meyrick over to play tennis.

Monday 3
Came back to school in 20 past train with Miss Wilson. Had a nice day. A pretty good science Exam. Saw Myfanwy Parry in train. Been eating cake nearly all day. Feeling pretty tired. Miss Hill coming to put out lights, so must close up shop - Susser Trormer. (in Q's adult hand: Traumer)

Tuesday 4
Had a real nice day. A pretty good music-lesson. Nice other lessons. Heard that England had declared war. But was a rumour, I think. Had a set of tennis with Edith Winter. She beat me 21:16. Went for a walk this afternoon through the Park & saw Lou Griffiths & Mr Pallister coming up Limestone Hill.

Wednesday 5

Had a nice day. Had a pretty fair music-lesson. Rather nice history exam, but don't know results yet. Nice English Literature. Played a set of tennis this afternoon against Edna Hadley but lost 16 (13?):21. Heard that Britain was at war but can't tell whether it true or not yet. Have to practise at six tomorrow, so must go to bed early. Hilda & I just short-sheeted Thelma's bed.

Thursday 6

Had a better day than I expected. Had a bonser German & also a nice science lesson. Had a rather nice Geography exam. Heard that the English fleet had "bottled up" the German fleet. Had a game of tennis with Marjorie Foote this afternoon won 21:16. Had pretty good Book-keeping lesson, but didn't get any home-letter.

Friday 7

Had a nice day. Had German Exam. Raining dreadfully heavily in the afternoon. Mummy drove in for me. We went down town & stayed shopping until about half-past six. Saw several people we knew. Saw Ted Palmer outside Pharmacy. Came home in the dark. Mummy had a bad cold.

Saturday 8

Daddy & Merv went to Brisbane to fix up the honey for the Exhibition. Mummy & I walked over to Appletons to have our photos taken with the dialogue people. Daddy & Merv stayed down in Brisbane all night.

Sunday 9

I fooled about all day. Morgan & Meyrick, Jim & Lou Griffith were over to play tennis in the afternoon. Morgan & Mick stayed for tea. Merv & Dad came home in the afternoon. Joey died.

Monday 10

Came back to school by train. Talking to Miss Connahun & then Miss Fox on Station. Prepared no home lessons hardly, but got through the day beautifully. Miss White went to Brisbane this afternoon. Everyone in IV, Low.IV & III got an impot. from Miss Cribb. Don't think it's fair. Feeling very sleepy but happy as only three more days.

101

Tuesday 11

Had a nice day. Miss Pitts' birthday, so we decorated our
room for her lesson. Had a pretty fair music-lesson this
morning. Had a nice walk this afternoon through the Park
& round a few streets. Pretty late, so I must get into bed.
Goodnight.

Wednesday 12

Had a fair day. Had a most cruel music-lesson this morning. This afternoon had rather nice English lesson. Played
Alice Andrews tennis match this afternoon & won 21-16. Not
too bad. Looking forward to tomorrow. Got a home letter
today, & don't know what to do about going home. Am in a
pretty big fix - per usual.

Thursday 13

Had a pretty fair day. Not extra good German lesson,
however. Came home from school by train with Jessie
Coogan. Had my mind made up to walk home, when
Mummy & Audrey turned up. Went to Farm for tea, &
squared Ivy to come to Exhibition, etc. with me. Came home
& stayed by ourselves all night as Daddy & Merv did not
turn up. They stayed at Uncle Dan's place.

Friday 14

Went to Bris. by 8 train with Ivy, did some shopping & went
out to Exhibition. Talking to Daddy, Merv, & Leila, then
struck Roy W. & G. Weise, who were with us all the afternoon.
At least Weise had to go, but Roy stayed. Missed our train
but caught one not long after. Merv. stayed at Uncle Dan's
again.

Saturday 15

Daddy went to Brisbane early. The rest of us got up late.
Mummy did a lot of cooking. Tom Waghorn over all the
morning. Mummy finished my evening coat. Daddy & Merv
came home at night. I went to bed before the others. I
found a nest with seven eggs in it.

Sunday 16

All from Farm & we three children went down to Harvey's to hear the graphophone in the afternoon. Mr Bowen & his brother were out. Meyrick was over to play tennis, and brought some chocolates.

Monday 17

Came back to school by train. Daddy took Audrey back to school. Heard news of a great war being fought. Had a pretty good day & had prep instead of hour-lesson science-lesson, as Mrs Pitts' father is dead. Did an awful lot of lessons tonight. Had none to prepare for tomorrow. Had a nice practice.

Tuesday 18

Had a lovely day. Pretty good music-lesson. Arithmetic Exam - & got 38. Had no science lesson, as Miss Pitts went away this morning, so we had prep instead. Had no walk this afternoon, so Thelma, Olive Bar & I were on the swings, which made us most frightfully sick.

Wednesday 19

Had a nice day. A fair music-lesson. Had rather bad English exam. Don't know whatever I'll get for my work. This afternoon could have gone to "Lost Days of Pompeii" at Lyric, but I didn't. I played three tennis matches and won one only. But played very good players. Week passing fairly quickly. Never got home-letter today, but suppose I will tomorrow. Miss White on duty this afternoon, & Miss Carmody this morning & tonight.

Thursday 20

Had a real nice German lesson. Had prep. instead of science lesson. Then had geography exam.. Think I did pretty well. Had a really nice English lesson this afternoon. Then had drawing Exam. Had pretty good book-keeping. Got no home-letter today. Packing up to go home.

Friday 21
I had a most frightful, awful, Cruel, monstrocious German exam! I don't think I'll ever recover from it. Mummy drove in for me about half-past three. We didn't go into town as Mummy had done all shopping before. Rain a little bit. Aunt Bess & Mr Scrogan came & stayed the night.

Saturday 22
Got up about half-past seven. Aunt Bess & Mr Scrogan went to Creek with Aunt Eve in morning. I fooled about all day, practised & did some of my lessons. Three Barns' kiddies over in morning & Tom came over in the afternoon.

Sunday 23
Morgan over in afternoon & we played tennis. Mr & Mrs Tom Smith & Mrs Copely were out. Aunt Bess & Mr Scrogan came again & stayed the night.

Monday 24
Got a most frightful cold. Came back to school this morning in train. Had most terrible science exam. Had rather nice other lessons. Got results of three exams., German 21, Algebra 27, & Geography 48. Not too bad. We three in this dorm. all got an impot - 200 hundred lines - from Miss Hill tonight, for making a row, so going to bed late.

Tuesday 25
Queenie Finegan ran away. Had a very easy day. Pretty nice music-lesson. Found I was in the marching & clubs at the concert, today. Went for a walk this afternoon & saw Barney Hogan & his wife flashing down Limestone Hill. Had prep. all the afternoon. Got the most frightful cold & headache.

Wednesday 26
Nothing special happened. Had pretty fair lessons. Got a letter from home this afternoon. My cold better a bit, but have got a very racking cough instead, which is worse, but saving on my hankies. Raining heavily this afternoon, so stayed in Boarders' sitting-room for the whole two hours after school. Look forward to getting up at six in the morning. Miss Pitt arrived back. Miss White on duty.

Thursday 27

Had a real good day, considering. Had a nice German & a nice science lesson. Had a most beautiful book-keeping lesson. My cold better, but my cough worse. Got a stiff neck in the bargain. A lot of girls went out tonight so we sat at our old table again for tea. It was just lovely. Going to pack so must hurry.

Friday 28

Had a nice day. Mummy called for me in the afternoon. We went down town & did some shopping, & came home. Ivy & Merv came to meet us & rode home with us. It was Ivy's birthday. She invited us in to her birthday tea but we couldn't stop. Daddy went to Brisbane for Audrey.

Saturday 29

Had a day of sewing - something new for me. Made my pincushion for the Bazaar. Also did a lot of sewing as I have to take back a fortnight's supply of clothes. Mr Chappell went to Bris. in the afternoon, so we were by ourselves at night.

Sunday 30

Played tennis in afternoon with Ivy, Merv & Meyrick. Played pretty badly. Finished my packing for school. Goodnight.

Monday 31

Came back to school by train, with other girls. Mummy took Audrey back to school. I had a rather nice day considering I didn't learn anything. Had a nice German lesson. I made some button-holes in a kit bag for the soldiers this afternoon. Been having some excitement over our evening-dresses.

Tuesday 1

Had a fair day. My music never turned up, so had no music except from Miss Cadogan. But hers were not natural! Said I might have had "courtesy" to tell her, etc., etc.. Very rainified today. Got as far as the gate in our walk, then turned back, so we danced in School Hall instead.

Wednesday 2
Had a most sponsiferous day. Got parcel of music, etc., & a letter from home today. Got a letter and invitation from Chrissie Bourke this morning, so quite lucky. I only practised half-an-hour today as my music only came this afternoon. Had a rather nice English exam.. For a wonder, I didn't have to have any sports this afternoon. Don't know what struck Miss Woods.

Thursday 3
Real nice day. Am having a lovely week, only that I cannot look forward to going home. Had a lovely German lesson. Am going to pack up now so must hurry. Most of the teachers have gone to a Ball tonight, so Miss Hill can't rouse tonight. Am looking forward to German exam tomorrow. It is pretty cold tonight.

Friday 4
Had German exam. this afternoon. Drilled in the afternoon until all-hours then going home with Phyllis, I met Mummy. She drove in almost to Wilsons. Phyllis & I went down town at night. Saw Mr James & two kiddies in town. Looking forward to Bazaar & Ball.

Saturday 5
Came up to school in the morning, where we drilled & arranged the stalls. In the afternoon came up to Bazaar with Phyllis. Had a good time. At night came up to Ball with Phyllis, Roy & Myrtle Chalmers. Had a scrummy time. Danced nearly all night but with girls mostly.

Sunday 6
Went to Church in morning. In the afternoon went to Cemetery with Nancy. At night went to Church again and Band Recital afterwards in the Park.

Monday 7
Came back to school once more. Bought a pair of gloves in town. Managed to scrape through lessons somehow until science lesson when I got 100 lines of my work to write out. Very sad!!! Had geography exam. & managed to scrape up 40 marks. Wrote a long letter home. Mummy sent me up a message from town with Mrs C & girls, saying she was alright.

Tuesday 8
Had a nice day. Had a beautiful music-lesson this morning. Told Miss Cadogan about Audrey. Had a fair science exam. but did something dreadfully. Got a note from Roy about the dance. Went for a walk this afternoon to the dressmaker's. Saw Blance Thomas in a bus.

Wednesday 9
Had a pretty fair day. Had a nice music-lesson, but not as nice as yesterday. Had a most glorious English lesson. Played four sets of tennis this afternoon with Alice Andrews against different kids - won three matches & lost the fourth. Most frightfully tired. Didn't get a letter from home so hope I'll get one tomorrow morning. Had some nice lemon-cream biscuits for supper tonight which is something extraordinary. (Made a startling discovery).

Thursday 10
Had a fair day considering. Had real nice German & Science lessons. Pretty fair other lessons. This afternoon did some book-keeping & were told that we have to have an exam. next Thursday - most dreadful. Didn't get a letter from home - horrible.

Friday 11
Had a nice day. Mummy drove in for me in the afternoon. I was excused from sports. We went into town & drove Phyllis down with us. As soon as we got into town, we met Chrissie therefore arranged for Saturday. Drove home in the dark. Audrey & Mary McCarthy also came home. It's lovely to get home.

Saturday 12
Had a nice time. Came up in the afternoon by train, met Chrissie & went straight to Boy's Grammar Sports. Then came back to Bourke's & got ready for evening at night, when I had a nice time - I do think.

Sunday 13
Feeling pretty tired. Ma's birthday. Went to Church in morning & night. Also Sunday School in afternoon. Also went for walk all round in the afternoon.

Monday 14 *Friendly Societies Day*

Came back to school from Bourke's. Mr Bourke carried my basket into town for me. Then I humped it through town & up Limestone Hill. Had a nice day of lessons. Got on alright in Science today. Hope this week passes as quickly as last. Miss Hill on duty so must hurry. Writing this Tues. morn. as Miss Hill put lights out before I finished.

Tuesday 15

Had a lovely music lesson. Then I studied for a while on back music room verandah instead of practising. It rained cats & dogs this afternoon, but just in time for our walk it cleared up, therefore didn't have muddy walk at all. Never got any home letter. I posted one home.

Wednesday 16

Had a fair day. All the class got an imposition from Miss Cribb in History Lesson. Had pretty good English. Had lovely music lesson. Like my new piece very much. Never got any letters or anything. Had to play basket-ball this afternoon & made an awful fool of myself. Tried to do some sewing, but didn't succeed very well. Just had an escapade in the bath-room with Thelma.

Thursday 17

Had a nice day considering. Had much better German lesson than I expected. Nice other lessons. This afternoon stewed book-keeping as hard as ever I could, & then found out it wasn't exam. after all. Dreadful. Thelma went home to get ready for her trip. Hilda & I went to gate to see her off. It rained for a while this afternoon.

Friday 18

Had pretty good German lesson. Had a rather nice day. Never went to practise in the morning, as knew I couldn't get a piano. Stayed at school, until nearly six o'clock, & then humped my basket down town, met Daddy, & talked to Nellie & Kate Stanley for a while, then drove home with Dad & Myfanwy in the sulky.

Saturday 19

Got up late. Worked in morning. MYfanwy went to Goodna for a drive with Dad. Fooled round & worked in afternoon. Went to bed pretty early. Helped catch six hens in the morning. Big procession of soldiers in Brisbane today.

Sunday 20

Went up to "Bees" in spring cart with Dad, Merv & Mif.. Then we all, including Mif. & Mr Chappel went for a picnic to Bush. Andy Smith's out in afternoon. Also Morg., Mey., Leonie, Ivy, Keith & Doris all over, with whom we played tennis.

Monday 21

Got a bong headache & sick in am. Drove down to Goodna with Mum & Myfanwy. Saw Myfan. off in 7.20 train, & waited for 7.55 train. Came up to school with Hilda & her cousin, Miss Cox. Was talking to Weise who was in next carriage. Had a rather nice day considering lessons. Had to umpire for basketball this afternoon. Feeling sick of myself, & everything else.

Tuesday 22

Had a nice day. Had a pretty good music lesson. Was very tired in morning - just about sick of school, myself & everything. Dying to do something desperate. I'm a mad ass! This afternoon had nice science lessons - experiments. Played with Nellie Caswell in monthly matches, & won every game until the last, against Ethel Nicholls & Dulcie Hodgson. Reckon we did extremely well.

Wednesday 23

Had a very nice day. Not feeling so down-in-the-dumpified today. Had an about-two-minutes music lesson this morning. Not a very nice history, but a glorious English literature lesson. Am still on my lonely-own tonight as Hilda has gone to Patriotic concert in town. Mrs O. went down town dressed all in red, white & blue - hideous. Had a game of tennis this afternoon with Muriel Collins.

Thursday 24
Had a very much nicer day than I expected. Had very nice German lesson, then a fair science lesson, added to which we had experiments after school. Miss Lilley went off about our Essays & about Patriotism. Never got a home letter. Most frightfully hot tonight.

Friday 25
Had a real nice day. Talked & laughed all last prep. Mummy called at school for me at nearly five o'clock. Thought she had forgotten my existence. Found Mummy had written & my letter must have gone astray. Got home fairly early. Nothing else startling happened. We only had tea, washed up & got into bed.

Saturday 26
Got up late. Worked hard nearly all day. Daddy & Merv went to Goodna. Kiddies from Farm came over in morning and afternoon. I sent them for butter in evening. Ma was very sick all afternoon.

Sunday 27
Got up late. In afternoon Mummy & I went over to Farm. Ma better. Morgan & Meyrick came over for tennis. Also two other men from Redbank or somewhere came to see Dad. Kiddies home with us in afternoon. Ivy & Merv played tennis also after sundown.

Monday 28
Ma went to Brisbane, so I went over to Farm & stayed with Ivy all day. We got kids off to school, & I did the housework. Then we made cream puffs, which we had for our dinner. They were something lovely. Ma drove back with Dan Carroll, then over to Mrs Ben Josey, who was sick. I came home when kiddies came. Mum & I went over at night. Ivy & I walked to Johnsons & Hilliers with all.

Tuesday 29
I drove over to Hall with Ivy & Mummy. While they were at dressmaking class, I went round that part of the Plains with the doll from Blind Girls. I got a good lot. Enjoyed day very much. Maud & Mrs Yarrow gave me a lovely bouquet & some bonser lime juice & cake. Drove home again & called at several places. Saw Tessie.

Wednesday 30

Went over to Farm again early as Ma had to go to Mrs. Ben Josey. Ivy & I got housework done in morning, then Ivy drafted in afternoon, while I read out Longfellow's "Tales of a Wayside Inn". We went down to Hillier's for Secret in morning & Ivy told me stories from the "Australasian". We had a lovely day. I came home about 4 o'clock with Daddy in spring-cart, & rode on the seat, too. Wrote some letters at last. Looked very much like rain several times today.

Thursday 1

Just fooled about all day. Mummy finished Audrey's silk dress. My report came, also the news that I have a h o l i d a y next Monday. Most scrabolocious!!! Haven't got over the shock yet. I was quite sick, sore hand & sciatica in my back over it, but they are slowly recovering from the shock. Played tennis with Ivy in afternoon.

Friday 2

Mummy did some sewing in morning. Then we did all the house out as we don't want to have to do any work tomorrow. Audrey & Miss Shepherd came home & I went to Farm to wait for them. Nothing special happened, except that as soon as I had finished watering plants, & bush-house, etc., a most gloriously heavy shower of rain came. Anyhow, I got over it, except that it doesn't look too promising for tomorrow night.

Saturday 3

Looked pretty rainified. Had breakfast in bed with Miss Shepherd & Audrey. Did housework in morning. Took all afternoon preparing for Social at night. We all went to Social, except Dad. Had a most gloriumptious time. Had my eye on someone, & after all didn't have a dance with this one. Sold bead work & doll's name announced.

Sunday 4

Rained hard in fits & starts all day. Audrey went over to Farm with Merv, and Ivy brought her back in afternoon. No one else came. Did my lessons.

Monday 5

Audrey & Miss Shepherd went back to school again as they did not have a holiday. It was pretty fine in morning, but in afternoon it rained very hard in fits & starts. Keith was over all day, & Ivy & Ivors came over for him in afternoon. I read nearly all afternoon. Mat. Kerwin came over at night & stayed until after ten. I went to bed about 9.30pm.

Tuesday 6

Came back to school again with Mummy in sulky. Had a pretty fair day but just simply hate being back at school again. Got on real well in my music-lesson & also in science lesson. Started reading "The Sky Pilot". Went for a walk in all the mud but it hardly rained at all. Had a heavy shower this afternoon.

Wednesday 7

Had a very nice day. Had a very fair music-lesson. Laughed a great deal. Had a nice English lesson also. Miss Lilley sent two girls out, & didn't even get in a temper for a wonder. But she has been pretty irritable all day. I played a lot of tennis this afternoon with Jessie Coogan & Muriel Collins. Also read some more "Sky Pilot". Got a letter from & wrote a letter to Chrissie. Looking forward eagerly to tomorrow, I don't think. Got most horrible German & Science.

Thursday 8

Had a very nice day & it passed very quickly. Had a lovely German lesson. Also a nice Science lesson. Per usual, Miss Cribb got on her dignity at history lesson, & we had to write out some. Has been raining fairly hard nearly all day. Had a most glorious book-keeping lesson. Miss White was on duty tonight, & I can hear Miss Pitts coming to put out the lights now.

Friday 9

Had a very nice day. Daddy rang up & said I had to come by train & wait for him in Goodna. Chrissie rang me up & Phyllis went to the phone instead of me. Told Chrissie to come by train. However she never came & I waited on the station until nearly six o'clock for her. Then I drove home with Daddy & found Mummy in bed with a strained back.

Saturday 10

Got up early & as Mummy was in bed did all the housework. Ivy came over & we washed & ironed all my things
& a few others. Rainified all day, & then we had a terrific storm in the evening. Two inches of rain fell. I had
a time cleaning up.

Sunday 11

Did all the housework. Mummy still in bed. In the afternoon
intended doing my lessons, but Mrs & Alie Hillier came &
stayed till night. Ma was over at dinner time. Had another
storm at night, & rain all day pretty well.

Monday 12

Had a nice day. Just simply hated leaving home. Mummy in
bed when I left. Came down to Goodna with Daddy then up
to school by train. Had nice lesson. Had a much nicer
history exam. than I expected. Played a 31-game of tennis
with Muriel Collins this afternoon & won. Had a bit of a
headache today, but nothing to speak about. Got slippers
which are too small. Wrote to Chrissie & Mummy.

Tuesday 13

Had a very lovely glorious music lesson this morning - best I
ever had. Miss Cadogan informed me that I am to try for
the Junior medal at Xmas. Had a very nice Science lesson.
IV & V had a lecture about our speech. I slammed a door on
my finger, & it's giving me "gip". Had a very nice walk this
afternoon. Am all alone tonight as Hilda has gone to a
lecture by Dr Crawford.

Wednesday 14 (Frances Wilson died.)

Had a fair day. Had a dreadful Arithmetic exam. &
capped it with a most horrible music lesson. Then had a
fair English exam. Had a pretty fair afternoon. Umpired
for basketball & read. Got two letters this morning - one
from home, & one from Thelma. My finger still sore.
Getting pretty late, so I must shut up. Got trillions of
lessons for tomorrow, although - one good thing - no
exams. I left no more news, so must shut up.

Thursday 15

Had a most frightful day - Horrible. Had rather nice - in fact, very nice - lessons. Had a very nice German lesson. Heard that little Frances Wilson was dead. Got an awful shock. Also Conny Kenny was found on the floor in her room in a faint at dressing bell tonight. Oh - most frightful. Never got any letters or anything, to break the monotony of things. Had a nice book-keeping lesson.

Friday 16

Came home from school by train. Drove home with Daddy in sulky, & then he went down & brought Miss Taylor & Miss Aird up. I walked home from Farm, while Ivy & Merv rode & carried the parcels. Alie Hillier had been over all day & the house was shifted upside down again but real nice just the same. I have to bunk on the couch in the sewing room for the weekend. Mr Chappell went to Brisbane.

Saturday 17

Got up very late. Had my breakfast in bed. Never woke even till late. Cleaned silver, etc. in morning. In the afternoon, it was threatening & raining a little. Ivors & Audrey came over for the afternoon. Intended going to Redbank Bazaar, but couldn't on account of rain. Mr Chappell came back at night.

Sunday 18

Got up late. Mr Carter from Redbank, & Mr Bryan or someone, a geologist came out, so took lunch up to Juillerat's old place, then climbed mountain. Meyrick over, so we all played tennis after we got home.

Monday 19

Drove down to Goodna with Daddy in cart. Mummy drove Miss Taylor & Miss Aird in sulky. Had a dreadful day. Had geography exam, then a fair German lesson. Middling English, then a cruel, cruel, Science Exam. Had game of tennis though to make up for it. Had to give it up, as it started raining very heavily. Phyllis came back to school. My finger pretty sore.

Tuesday 20

Had a pretty fair day. Had just a per-usual Music lesson. Got up with a headache, which increased all day pretty well, but a little better now. Had a game of tennis this afternoon. Then on top of that we went for an awfully long walk right down to the River & back. Feeling most frightfully tired. May McKee in the hospital with a bad headache.

Wednesday 21

Had the most frightful music lesson I ever had since I've been here. Had fair to middling English lesson. Pretty bad History. I got a letter from Chrissie Bourke by Edith Winlaw. Also this afternoon got a letter from Mummy, saying North people were coming down. Looking forward to getting home. Had a most glorious game of tennis with Jessie Coogan & Muriel Collins. I won first but lost second. Wrote to Thelma, but haven't posted it.

Thursday 22

Winton people arrived in Brisbane. Had a very nice day considering. Had a very nice German lesson. Got results of Science Exam. & I got 27 - the highest being only 37. Also got results of Geography - got 45 - highest being 46, so didn't do badly. Had pretty bad History lesson. Fairly good English. Then we ended up with Drawing Exam - pretty bad per usual. Played tennis on new courts with Muriel Collins & Thelma Graham. Looking forward to German Exam.

Friday 23

Had a fair day. Had nice morning, then had a pretty awful exam. (German) in V form this afternoon. Don't know what to expect for results, I'm sure. Drove home with Mummy & Chrissie. Posted a letter to Thelma in afternoon. All Winton folk came up from Goodna in Hillier's cab. They are awfully nice - especially Coralie. Audrey never came home.

Saturday 24

Mummy & Merv went to Brisbane early in morning, & brought Audrey home with them in afternoon. Chrissie & I fooled round all the morning & in afternoon went to Farm. At night, Aunties Laura, Audrey & Rosie & Ivy came over - not forgetting Coralie, whom I put to sleep at night, etc.

Sunday 25
Got up late. In afternoon played tennis with Aunties Audrey & Ivy, Chrissie, Morgan, Meyrick & Lou Griffith. Had a bit of music at night.

Monday 26
Came back to school with Chrissie as far as East Ipswich. Found, to my great surprise, Thelma in the train. Audrey went back to school with Daddy. Had a pretty fair day of lessons. Had an awful History exam.. Got results of German exam. I got the grand sum of 28. Am feeling very proud of myself. Had drawing instead of singing this afternoon.

Tuesday 27
Had a very nice day. Had a pretty fair music lesson - I have forgiven Miss Cadogan now. Had a lovely Algebra lesson. Miss Cribb as much as told me I was going into V form. Had pretty fair science lesson - had an hour, because we had to stay in for ¼ hour from Miss Cribb's roll-call. Went for a walk to Park this evening. I walked with Thelma.

Wednesday 28
Had a rather nice day. My music lesson started beautifully, but collapsed. Had very nice History lesson, for a wonder. Then had English exam. Liked it fairly well - but not parsing & analysis. Had pretty nice algebra lesson & prep.. Then played tennis at 4.45p.m. with Thelma T., Jessie Coogan & Muriel Collins. Until then I read "Lamb's Tales from Shakespeare", & liked them very much. Got a letter from Mummy.

Thursday 29
Had a nice day I think - oh rubbish. Had fair German lesson. Then pretty good Science lesson. Very nice Geography & History lessons. The Miss Lilley was in a most glorious humour for English. Had a beautiful lesson. Had a very nice last prep. Then played tennis on new courts with Jessie Coogan, Muriel Collins, & Thelma T. Mr Jones didn't turn up for book-keeping, so Thelma & I had lessons to ourselves.

Friday 30

Had a rather nice day. Had algebra exam. Think I did better than last time. Didn't have any other interesting events. Waited for Mummy for about two hours in the afternoon. Thought Daddy was coming, but it was Mummy. And I didn't rouse either (indecipherable insert). Got home at last. Merv was alright after his operation. Going down again tomorrow. Ivors came over.

Saturday 31

Mummy & Merv went down by 8 train to Brisbane. Therefore Ivors & I were left at home to keep house, which we did beautifully. About dinnertime Auntie Rosie came over, and I had finished all work then. In afternoon, Aunties Audrey & Ivy came over to play tennis, then A.A. & L.R. went to dance in Goodna at night.

Sunday 1

Mr Chappell away all day. In afternoon, Farm people came over, also Meyrick, to play tennis. I never played, did lessons instead. Little Jimmie Campbell's birthday.

Monday 2

Came back to school again. Drove to Goodna with Mum & Merv who went to doctor in Brisbane again. Had two exams – Geography & Science – Don't think I did too badly. Got results of Algebra – 36. My wisdom tooth coming through alright. Thelma was sick this morning, & Hilda this afternoon, but both alright now, so no worry.

Tuesday 3

Had an middling good music lesson. Got some new studies. Then had nice other lessons for a wonder. Then Thelma & I read until walk-time. Had a walk down towards the River, but never went right there. Miss Hill just came in to stop Hilda & me romping, but was a ducky darling about it.

Wednesday 4

Had a nice day considering. Had fair to middling music lesson. Miss Cadogan showed me some nice postcards. Had a nice History lesson. Then had a very nice English lesson. Had nice rest of lessons. Mrs O' held her Belgian affair this afternoon & lots of people were up here. I think I saw Mrs Grimley, but she didn't seem to know me, so I never spoke. Umpired for a four match this afternoon, & then played tennis for about an hour. It is most frightfully hot.

Thursday 5

Had a lovely day. Not an extra-good German lesson. But very nice other lessons. Looked at war-pictures in some magazine of Miss Cribb's until 5 o'clock. Then had a nice book-keeping lesson. From about ¼ to 7 until 20 past 7, we had some privates. Some were very nice. Got a home letter. Some girl friend of sixth form is staying tonight - Dolly somebody or other.

Friday 6

Had an awful, most terrible German Exam.. Then Ruby & I went home by train, & Mummy drove us out from Goodna. Had a good day excepting the German Exam. I went into Farm, & at night we washed up, while Mummy did a bit to the dark blouse she is making me. It is going to be nice, I think. Feeling pretty tired.

Saturday 7

Got up late, after having breakfast in bed. Did a lot of work, while Mummy finished making my blouse. I like it real well. Merv & Ruby dipped the cows in afternoon. At night, Mummy drove Aunties Audrey & Rosie to a dance in Hall. Only four ladies there, & ever so many men, but danced all night.

Sunday 8

Got Mummy's breakfast & did most of work before she got up. In afternoon, Aunties Audrey, Rosie, & Ivy came over to play tennis. I did some lessons.

Monday 9

Came back to school in train with Ruby. Daddy drove us to Goodna. Had a pretty bad German lesson - results of exam. Had alright other lessons & had history exam. It wasn't too bad. Mummy wrote to Miss White about Doreen coming for a week-end. Thelma & I played a 3pm game of tennis this afternoon on old courts. Nothing else seriously funny happened, so must shut up.

Tuesday 10

Had a pretty dreadful music-lesson. Then had nice other lessons, including Science, when we had some lovely experiments. Thelma & I talked to Phyllis W. & Doreen M., & then Enid Lord & Dulcie H., until quarter to five. Then we went for a lovely walk.

Wednesday 11

Had a very nice day. Had a pretty fair music lesson. Then enjoyed algebra very much. Had a lovely English exam - so I thought, but alas! For my thoughts, - they were absolutely all wrong. Had an alright History lesson - better than usual. Played tennis with Thelma this afternoon, & then read the rest of time until tea. Writing this in dark, so must shut up.

Thursday 12

Had an awfully exciting day. Started German lesson this morning when Inspector came, so we only had a little bit of German then Inspection for Science, & also Geography - when he asked us the most awful questions. Had a very nice History lesson, but Inspector in for English & Drawing. Then Miss Woods called the "two models of energy", i.e. Thelma & Me, to basket-ball, but played tennis instead. Rained a bit this afternoon. Then Thelma had book-keeping exam..

Friday 13

Had a nice day. Had Algebra exam. The Inspector corrected & took his marks from the exam. Horrible! Had an alright German lesson. Then Doreen & I drove home with Mummy in sulky. Had a nice drive. Especially with apples and bananas. Stopped at Farm for a few minutes. Girls came over at night, & we had a musical evening. Also great on the tango.

Saturday 14

Got up late & Doreen & I got our own breakfast. Merv & Mummy went down by early train to Brisbane & brought Audrey home in the afternoon. Ivy came over in morning & stayed all day. Aunties Audrey & Rosie came over for tennis in afternoon & had music at night. Audrey went home with them & stayed all night.

Sunday 15 *Ruby's birthday*

Got up awfully late. Merv went over for Audrey about dinnertime. Mr Kerwick & another fellow drove out in afternoon. Also Auntie Audrey & Ivy, Morgan & Meyrick came over for tennis. Mr McMahon also over. Morgan & Meyrick stayed for some music.

Monday 16

Drove down in Cart to Goodna. Daddy & Audrey went down to Brisbane by the 7.20 down train, & we went by same up train. Saw Elwyn Parry but couldn't see Myfanwy. Then when walking up to school, Ted Palmer flashed past in a motor & wouldn't even look at me. Had an awful school day. Never did such an awful Science. The Inspector still here, but I didn't have him at all today. Had pretty bad Geography exam..

Tuesday 17

It was a most frightfully hot day. I nearly melted - only that I was too substantial, I would have done so. Had a much better music lesson than I expected. Then had a pretty nice Arithmetic exam. Miss Cribb paid us compliments all Algebra lesson. Had experiments all Science lesson. Had a pretty good walk through park.

Wednesday 18

Had an alright day. Had not-extra-good music lesson. Had a pretty nice English lesson. Not a good History lesson by any means. Played tennis nearly all the afternoon, first with Thelma T., & afterwards with Thelma Graham & May Smith joined us. Then at a ¼ to 5, Hilda played Thelma T. & me. She won, of course, about 31-14. Got results of Arithmetic Exam. tonight. I managed to get 34. Got an awful day tomorrow. Got a home letter.

Thursday 19

Managed to scrape through the day beautifully. Had a very nice Grammar lesson. Then all had to stay in for Miss Pitts in Science lesson, & then a pretty dreadful Drawing Exam - last exam this year. Never had Book-keeping exam..

Friday 20

My last day in Upper Fourth. I went down to Goodna by train, & then after visiting Harnell's, waited on station from 20 to 5 until 25 to 7, for the trip train. I was so wild because I couldn't go. I don't reckon it's at all fair. Nothing very wonderful happened else. Saw most of my old Plains friends again - especially Maud, who gave me a shell.

Saturday 21

Got up awfully late. Mum did also. We both read & slept nearly all the morning. Then Mum did some cooking in the afternoon. Pretty hot day, so wouldn't be surprised if there's a storm before morning. Ma is pretty sick. None of girls came over today or tonight.

Sunday 22

Got up early. Pretty big storm last night. Mum & I went to Farm in a long shower in afternoon. Morgan was over to play tennis & stayed for a bit in the evening.

Monday 23

Came back to school by train. It is my first day in Fifth Form. So far I have liked it tremendously. Nearly dead with English for tomorrow all the same. Had a most angelic, beautiful, sweet dream of an English lesson today. Also had a pretty extra-special nice German lesson this afternoon. Had nice other lessons, am not feeling very tired, but must shut up.

Tuesday 24

First day of Junior & Senior. Papers were not too bad. Got letter from Roy W.. Had a pretty nice day. Had a nice English lesson, & also a pretty fair hour History lesson. Then practised & had prep. this afternoon. Read - fooled really - until walk time, when we went through the Park & around a bit.

Wednesday 25

Had a much better day than I expected to have. Had a pretty nice History lesson, although we had tons of it. Had very nice Science lesson - had mostly experiments. Alice A. & I did German this afternoon until Miss Pitts came along. I played tennis at 5, with at first - Alice A. & Thelma T. - then with Thelma. We were talking to Muriel Summerville over the fence for a good bit, when Miss White sent a girl to send us away. Tons of lessons for tomorrow.

Thursday 26

Had a lovely Chemistry lesson. Had a much better German lesson than I expected. Then had a lovely English lesson for hour lesson. Has been storming all the afternoon & is still thundering. Had a nightmare of a Book-keeping exam. Can't possibly get any marks for it. Got no home letter. Got tons of lessons for tomorrow.

Friday 27

Got through the day all right. Had to do some awful German, but mine turned up with "Very Fair". Had a nice English lesson. Came to Goodna by train, and, after visiting the nearest lolly-shop, waited on station for Mummy, who brought Audrey & Miss Littley up for the Social. Saw Mr Horn - like him very much. Girls over for some music at night.

Saturday 28

Got up pretty middling early. Auntie Audrey came over & stayed all day. Walked all over Creek with Ivy in afternoon looking for cows. Pretty dull all day & then started raining in the evening. Mat. Kerwin didn't come for us, so we went over to Social in the cart with the Goodna boys. Had every dance at the Social. Afterwards Redbank boys kicked up a row, but all got home safely.

Sunday 29

Got up late. Auntie Audrey & Audrey came over in morning, & the rest in the afternoon. Morgan came over to play tennis. We got a native bee's hive out of a tree. Had some music at night.

Monday 30

Came to Goodna in sulky with Daddy & Merv, then up by train. Had a very nice day. Had a nice English lesson, & also lovely German one. Was never so stiff & sore in my life -it is awful. Got some lovely (!) history for tomorrow, & don't know anything about it. It's awful, all the Home people going to the Carnival in Brisbane, & poor me stewing for all I'm worth.

Tuesday 1

Felt most frightfully tired this morning. Not nearly so stiff & sore as yesterday, though. Had - per usual - a most fearful music lesson. Don't know how I'm going to live till holidays. Had a very nice History lesson. Had the 1st week this year - a very long one too. There was a big fire down at Cribb's - great excitement - Think I will get out of my Medal piece, if I can.

Wednesday 2

Had a very nice day - but have a crick in my shoulder today. Had a very nice History lesson. Also had a lovely Chemistry lesson this afternoon - we had all experiments. Played tennis for a while this afternoon with Thelma T., Alice A. & Doris Woodward. Then read out to Thelma for rest of time, so now have another complaint - a sore throat. Am nearly killed with lessons for tomorrow. I'm sure I don't know how I am going to survive till Friday even - much less this day week.

Thursday 3

Had a nice day. Had a lovely English lesson, also beautiful Chemistry, & History & German lesson - latter had about ten minutes to spare. Read this afternoon until a quarter to five. The had a nice book-keeping lesson - and - oh! dear! - got results of my exam - 55 whole marks. Getting quite excited about going home. Packing a lot of extra things for holidays.

Friday 4

Had a nice day - the last Fridays school this year - scribocious. Miss Cadogan relieved my mind telling me I had no chance for the Medal (music). Drove home with Mummy in sulky. Arranged to go in to school tomorrow for my music exam. Not looking forward to it extra much. Rained fairly hard early this morning. No more news.

Saturday 5
Went to Ipswich by 11 train. Did shopping, & then met Miss Wilson, & went up there until time to come to school. Then came up with Phyllis & made a fool of myself at exam.. Then came back to Goodna by train, where Mummy & Jimmy were waiting for me in the sulky. Came down in train with Allan Bourke.

Sunday 6
Did an awful lot of work - but nothing to what Mum did. Willie McKeon & Campbell girls over in the afternoon. A bit of a storm in evening. Mr Chappell came back.

Monday 7
Came back to school in train. Ivy & Auntie Rosie went to Brisbane to meet May Williams. I had a pretty good day. Miss Lilley in a rat this morning, but was alright in our form. Had a real nice German lesson - last one this year. Miss White on duty tonight so must hurry into bed. A big thunder storm this afternoon, & weather been taking fits of raining ever since.

Tuesday 8
Had a nice day. Had a lovely music lesson. Miss Cadogan laughed at my mistakes in music exam. Had a very nice History lesson - we got lectured at about half the time about leaving school, etc. - Miss White got quite worked up. Getting frightfully excited about going home. Looking forward to a lovely day tomorrow. Last whole day's school.

Wednesday 9
Had a beautiful day. Had a very nice History lesson. Then had a lovely afternoon. Had only morning school. Then found to the surprise of my life that I had got two prizes - Geography & Junior Book-keeping. Had some bonser dances tonight - Lancers, Waltz, Mazurka & Twostep. Also had some lovely fooling, but found to my disgust & mortification - something, too late, because I was too good. I think it's frightfully mean - but looking forward to tomorrow. No more school this year.

Thursday 10
Girls had midnight supper last night, as most had to be up by 6 o'clock this morning, but Thelma & I slumbered on until seven. Then fooled around all the morning until people came. Then we had a glorious lunch & then went in for distribution of prizes. Ivy, Mummy & I went to Wilson's for dinner. Then we all motored up to Boy's Breaking-Up in the afternoon. Had a very nice day. Came home in the late evening. Got two prizes. Ivors came home with us. Girls were over.

Friday 11
Got up very late. Mummy went to Brisbane to bring Audrey home. Ivors stayed with me all day to keep me company. We fooled around all day, typewriting, reading, playing piano, & all sorts of things. Mum & Audrey arrived home about 5 o'clock. Ivy & May Williams also came over, & they & Merv marked & did up the tennis court. The report of our breaking-up was in the paper.

Saturday 12
Got up late. Didn't do much work. Ivors still here. Morgan came over in afternoon for some tennis. He told us the Goodna boys weren't coming out. We all went over to Mrs Gorman's Social in our sulky & Mat. Kerwin's buggy. Uncle Dan came up & went over to Social as well. I had a pretty rotten time.

Sunday 13
Audrey came back from Farm. Mr & Mrs Smith, Lou Griffiths, Mr Clayton, Uncle Dan (who stayed here Saturday night) & Farm Girls were over in afternoon. A. & I read nearly all afternoon under the trees.

Monday 14
First real holiday - and also washing day. I read to Audrey in the morning, nevertheless. Then we took down curtains, changed beds, etc., after dinner, & fooled around rest of day, doing nothing very wonderful. Getting on well with "Dombey & Son". We like it very much. Mummy's arms are still very sore. Pretty hot day - the days are very summery just now. My report has not come yet - expecting it. Audrey Barns came over.

Tuesday 15
Mummy washed curtains, etc. in the morning while Audrey
& I did some housework. I cleaned every window in the
house, I believe, upstairs & downstairs. Audrey was over at
the Farm nearly all day. My report came - about the best I
have had yet. Mummy ironed in the afternoon & finished at
night. We arranged about our concert.

Wednesday 16
The most frightfully hot day we've had this summer. It was
108° in the shade. I got an attack of temporary dazedness
in the morning. I read out "Pollyanna" to Audrey most of
the afternoon. Then about five o'clock a big storm threatened but only a little rain came. Mr Lewis & kiddies were
here for a while until the storm cleared up a bit. The week is
passing very quickly, & I can't for the life of me put down
any news or whatever you call it in here, so must shut up.

Thursday 17
Still a hot day. Ma came over in the morning to see Mum's
arms - worse than she expected. Ma went back after dinner &
took Audrey over with her to stay the night. Ivy & Auntie Rosie
came over late in afternoon to play tennis. I had a lovely
afternoon, arranging postcards, painting, reading, etc.. We
arranged to go to town tomorrow if Mum's arms were better,
to get Xmas things. Got a surprising letter from Miss Wilson.

Friday 18
Mummy stayed in bed all day instead of going to town, so I
had to keep house. I did all housework in the morning.
Then Merv & I cooked in afternoon - made biscuits, pudding
& custard. Ivy over with dresses in afternoon. Ma sent over
some things for tea with Evie Hillier. A big storm threatened,
but passed almost right over. I wrote to Vera at night.

Saturday 19
Mummy got up & intended going straight back to bed, but
stayed up until about 4 o'clock. Daddy went to Ipswich, &
got groceries, etc.. Audrey came home from Farm with Ma.
Then we read until dark, & went to bed early. Ivors &
Audrey were over for dinner.

Sunday 20

Worked all the morning. Then I played tennis nearly all the afternoon - played 4 ½ sets. Ivy & Auntie Rosie, Morgan & Meyrick & Garnet Hillier were over this afternoon.

Monday 21

One week is over - worse luck. The mail caused great excitement this morning. We three children got Christmas boxes from Byrnes. Thelma & Ivors were over for a while. Struck on surprise party - only guessed. Worked in kitchen all the afternoon - cleaned down dressers, etc.. Audrey & I played tennis, went for a walk, & then bicycle ride, & ended up by getting giggles badly.

Tuesday 22

Aunties Audrey & Rosie came over early in morning & washed & ironed. Went home about 5 o'clock. I cleaned knives, silver, & worked terribly hard all day. Daddy drove Auntie Laura to Goodna & came home with news there was a surprise party tonight. However, we bustled round, but only the Campbell girls, Meyrick J., J. & P. Small & N. Gibson arrived. I received a few Xmas cards. Had an alright time at surprise party.

Wednesday 23

Auntie Laura, Coralie & Ivors stayed all night last night. Ivors & I slept on a mattress on the sewing room floor. Worked hard all day. Ironed, washed floors, & all sorts of thing. Expected surprise party, but it did not come after all. There were signs of a storm tonight - plenty of thunder & lightning. I wish to goodness there was not so much to write in Wednesday as I don't know for the life of me what to write. So I will say goodnight.

Pages for Dec 24-31 are disintegrating, with parts missing.......

Thursday 24

Worked or fooled round in morning.   ?? went to Goodna & came home about ? o'clock. Mummy, Merv & I went to ? in afternoon. Auntie Audrey & Aunt Rosie rode in & were with us nearly all the time. We stayed in for a while at night. I saw a lot of people I knew at night.

Friday 25

Got up & got tidy. Lou Griffiths came over in morning to see Daddy. Had a bonser Xmas dinner - just the five of us. Merv & I started to play tennis in afternoon, but it rained pretty hard. It cleared up afterwards, however. All except Daddy went over to Farm for Xmas tea. Mr Waghorn was there & came home with us & stayed the night. Came home late.

Saturday 26

Mrs Lewis, family, & friends came out to spend the day & have a picnic, etc.. Arrived about 10.30am & went home about 6 pm. All Farm people came over as well. Spent day in music, reciting, tennis, etc.. Had 27 visitors altogether.

Sunday 27

Fooled around in morning. In afternoon Meyrick came over for tennis. Mick Wilson got half-way out but bike broke. Aunties Rosie & ? & Mr. Waghorn over. Mat. Kerwin over at night.

Monday 28

???? stormy day. Daddy went to Goodna in morning. No mail. Didn't ? in morning. Rained pretty hard just after dinner, then cleared up. I read out "Dombey & Son" to Audrey nearly all the afternoon. Harold Younger & Muriel rode up in afternoon. We said goodbye as he is going to the war. Audrey fell head over heels in love with him.

Tuesday 29

Mum washed & primus blazed up. Joe Gard. over to see Daddy. Merv went to Goodna. I got a p.c from Eric & a letter from Thelma Graham. I read out to Audrey nearly all the afternoon. Ivy came over in afternoon to play tennis. We had a few games & fooled rest of time. Merv rode over to Farm with Ivy on bicycle. Tom came over & stayed the night. It looked very much like a storm.

Wednesday 30

Mr Waghorn went to Brisbane & we got up late. Mummy went over to Farm in morning, & brought Ivors home with her, so have both Ivors & Tom over now. Read out to Audrey, & gathered, & peeled pears in afternoon. Harold Y. & Billie H. left Goodna for their "Encounter" this morning. Mummy, Merv & I played tennis in the evening. Doctor came out to see Eva - thinks it is typhoid. Muriel & Morgan rode over with papers for Daddy.

Thursday 31

Mummy sewed all day. In the morning ??? knives, silver, & did some ??????. Didn't knock ourselves up. ?????? came over in afternoon. Ivy stayed & p?????? ??? & Audrey & Ivors went to Harvey's. Thelma ? came over & went home with Ivy. Aunties Rosie & Ivy went to Ipswich at night. Am looking forward to two ice-creams. Read a bit of "Dombey & Son" in bed this morning. Threatened to storm this afternoon & rained in fits & starts all day.

Page 136: 1915 Diary

Got up earlier than any day yet in the holidays

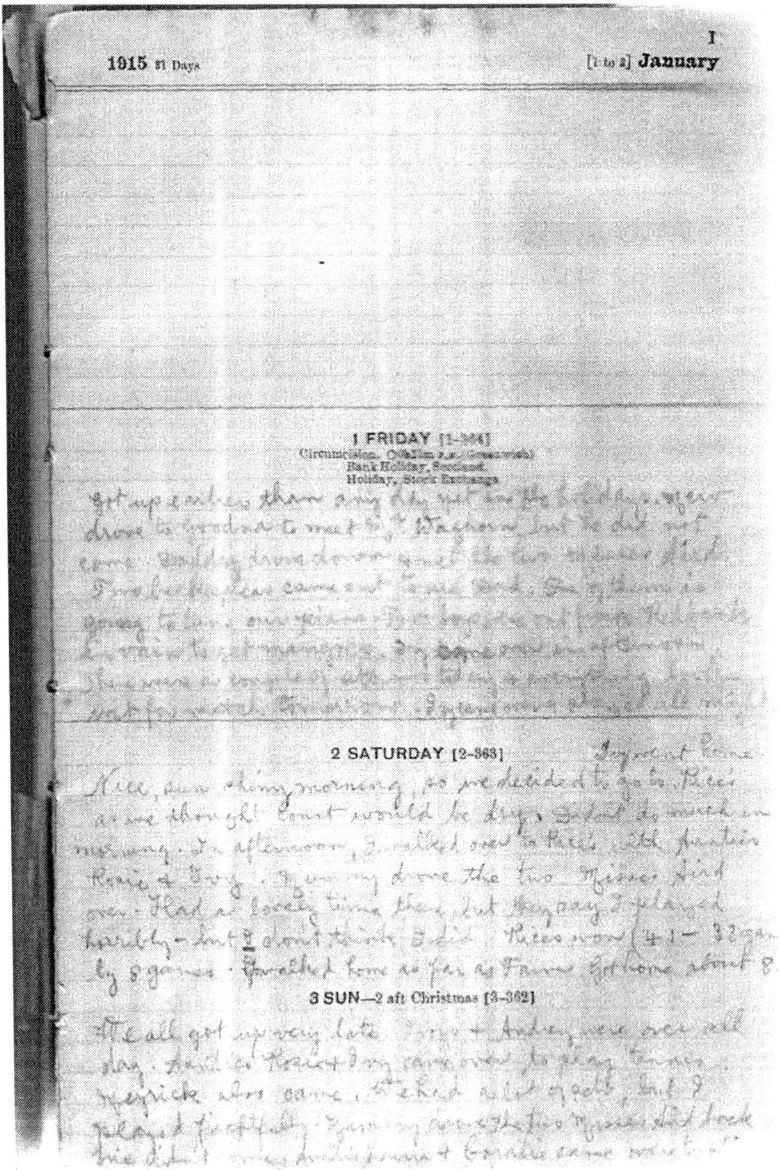

1 FRIDAY [1-364]
Circumcision. Old Jan 1 a.s. (Greenwich)
Bank Holiday, Scotland.
Holiday, Stock Exchange.

2 SATURDAY [2-363]

3 SUN—2 aft Christmas [3-362]

1915
Diary

Friday 1
Got up earlier than any day yet in the holidays. Merv drove to Goodna to meet Mr Waghorn, but he did not come. Daddy drove down and met the two Misses Aird. (At least one was a teacher at Audrey's school.) Two beekeepers came out to see Dad. One of them is going to tune our piano. Two boys were out from Redbank in vain to get mangoes. Ivy came over in afternoon. There were a couple of storms today and everything looks wet for match tomorrow. Ivy (Campbell) came over and stayed all night.

Saturday 2
Nice, sun-shining morning, so we decided to go to Rice's as we thought the court would be dry. Didn't do much in morning. In afternoon I walked over to Rice's with Auntie's Rosy and Ivy. Mummy drove the two Misses Aird over. Had a lovely time there, but they say I played horribly - but I don't think I did. Rices won (41-33 game) by 8 games. I walked home as far as Farm. Got home about 8.

Sunday 3
We all got up very late. Ivors and Audrey (Barns) were over all day. Aunties Rosie and Ivy (Campbell) came over to play tennis. Meyrick also came. We had a lot of sets, but I played frightfully. Mummy drove the two Misses Aird back. Evie didn't come. Auntie Laura and Coralie (Campbell) came over to stay.

Monday 4
Got up much earlier than usual. Mummy sewed all day, making me a new dress. I wrote to Eric, and Mum answered some ads from Manly. Dad and Merv went to Brisbane. Audrey B. came over to stay for a few days. Fred Butler came to see Dad. Lou Griffiths came over in evening with rest of ticket money. Ma came over just before tea, and stayed for a while. Coralie and Auntie Laura got a bee-sting each this afternoon. Coralie's very bad, just near her eye.

Tuesday 5
Got up about same time as usual. Mummy and Audrey
drove to town (Ipswich) about ten o'clock.. Eric Hebden
arrived home with Merv this morning. Auntie Laura made
some cocoanut ice. Ivy came over this afternoon to ask me
to go to Sandgate tomorrow, and take Audrey home. There
were signs of a big storm this evening. Got and answered
invitations from Chrissie (Bourke).

Wednesday 6
Malcie Campbell was married. Awfully hot day.
Went down to Sandgate with Aunties Audrey and Ivy and
Ivors, Audrey, Keith (Barns) and Thelma. Ivy took
Thelma to her mother. We bathed and walked around
and rested etc, all day. Went down by 8.15am train, and
back to Brisbane 3.22pm train. Mrs McDonald brought
Edna to train and we brought her home. Went to Valley
pictures in Brisbane and did a tiny bit of shopping. Left
Brunswick Street by 6.09pm train and drove home from
Goodna with Daddy, who had waited for us. He went to
Board meeting. There was a terrific storm in afternoon.

Thursday 7
Got up very late. Didn't do much before dinner. In afternoon, cleaned shoes ironed, etc,. Mum ironed nearly all
day, notwithstanding the fact of it being her birthday. I
am very sunburnt from yesterday. Got a favourable letter
from Mrs Curtis about Manly. I ironed for over two hours in
the afternoon. Ma came over in the afternoon. Ivy also
rode up to wish Mummy many happy returns. Read ever so
much of "Dombey and Son".

Friday 8
Got up about eight o'clock. Read a lot of "Dombey and
Son" before we got up. Then read some more before dinner
and finished the book after dinner. Between 2 and 3
o'clock we started getting ready for town and left about 4.
Got in after six and Chrissie (Bourke) was waiting for us.
She took Audrey and me home to her place. We had a
musical evening - Audrey played mostly. (Audrey would
have been 12 years old.)

Saturday 9

Got up extra early for us. Helped Chrissie wash up etc., for a while. Then Myrtle and I took turns of reading out to Audrey for the rest of the morning. In the afternoon, Chrissie, Myrtle (Bourke), Audrey and I went down town for an icecream. Chrissie and I shouted in turns. We watched a wedding party. Also went to Allen's. Hilda and Walter over at night.

Sunday 10

Got up later than usual. Went to church in the morning, then went to Sunday School in afternoon whre Mr Bourke was awfully nice to Audrey. Then completed day by going to church at night.

Monday 11

Left Ipswich by the 10 to 7 train. Chrissie saw us off. Also Walter was in same train. Met Mummy, Merv and Auntie Rosie in Goodna. Came on to Manly then. Had a couple of walks, then had dinner. Didn't do much in afternoon except read out to Audrey. Then about 5 o'clock had a bath. After tea, we were introduced to rest of boarders. Had electric battery of Mr Smith's until about half past nine.

Tuesday 12

Had a bathe about seven o'clock. Plenty of jelly fish, so I didn't stay in long. Smiths went this morning. We got possession of their room. Another lady came into ours in afternoon. Eric was up a couple of times to-day. Mrs Hebden and Mrs and Stanley Pringle came up to visit us this afternoon. We had a bathe after they went. Had late tea and then went to the moving pictures. Mummy wrote letters to Daddy and Ma.

Wednesday 13

The tide was lovely this morning and only saw one jelly fish, so had a lovely bathe. Eric was with Merv nearly all day. Mrs Jacobson went to town. Audrey, Isabel and I went out shopping in the morning. Then came home and read until (late) dinner time. It rained in the afternoon, so had to stay inside, and read or talked. In the evening, I took Audrey for a paddle. Then went for a bit of a walk with Mummy, Isabel, Mrs MacDonell and Val Howard and nephew. Had a bit of a concert at night, and George Jacobson's electric battery. Holidays passing quickly.

Thursday 14

Got up late and had a bathe. No jelly-fish at all this morning. Went for a walk to jetty, read out under a tree to Audrey for a while, then joined by Mummy and Mrs and Lennie McDonnell. Read nearly all the afternoon, then in evening went for mail but as we (Audrey and I) were too early, went for a walk to station, where we were greatly surprised to get Ivy and Keith. Anyhow, we brought them home, and after a few walks etc., Ivy, Merv and I went to pictures at night.

Friday 15

Got up late and after breakfast a while, went in for a bathe. Water very rough and weather windy and a little showery. Ivy, Keith, Audrey and I went shopping and on jetty in the morning. Also went for a bit of a walk round towards Wynnum South and on the sands just before tea. We read for a while at night, then finished up with cards.

Saturday 16

Had a lovely bathe in the morning, then had breakfast and the ice-cream man came along, so had two each. There was a boat race in the afternoon. We played cards and watched it a bit from the house at the same time. Then we went for a walk on to the jetty. At night we went to the pictures, which were beautiful.

135

Sunday 17

May Hebden arrived in morning, just as we were going to church, but it rained so we didn't go. Vera and Percy Harwood came in the afternoon and Bob came to see us at night, so had quite a lot of visitors.

Monday 18

Got up pretty late. Mrs McDonnell recited to us. Had a nice bathe about eleven o'clock. The water was smoother than it has been since we came down here. Learned to float and loved it. Read nearly all afternoon, then in evening Ivy, Audrey, and I went to the post office and station on affairs of business. Ivy was not well all day. We had some of George Jacobsen's battery at night.

Tuesday 19

Ivy and I took castor oil and at the seaside, the vilest thing ever happened. Isn't it sad! Ivy and I stayed in bed until ???? 1 o'clock when we went in for a bathe. Uncle Dan, who was down, also had a swim. We went to bed for rest of afternoon and in evening Ivy, Keith, Audrey and I went to post office. Some went to pictures tonight but we played cards at home instead.

Wednesday 20

Merv and I went to station with Ivy and Keith to catch 7.35 train. Herb also came up before train went out. Just read and generally fooled round all the morning. Same in afternoon. Mummy packed and cleaned out room nearly all day. She wasn't very well - wish there had been some more medicine left. I might have had my revenge. Audrey and I went for a walk on sands in evening and gathered shells. Played cards for a bit at night. Mum and George J. had bad headaches. Went to bed early.

Thursday 21

After a very pleasant journey and a halt in Brisbane, we arrived home in time for dinner. Met Mrs G. at Corinda. Jim Rice was here when we came back - also a big water-melon. Unpacked in afternoon. Mummy, Audrey and I went over to Farm in afternoon to say goodbye to Auntie Rosie. We went to bed pretty early. I stayed up a bit later than the rest. Mum had a headache and not feeling well.

Friday 22
Pottered round among the pot-plants with mummy all morning. Auntie Rosie went up north to an outlandish place (Einasleigh). Mum and I washed in the afternoon. Ben Griffiths came for some mangoes. Dad and Merv went to town in afternoon. Looked "showerified" all day today. We all went to bed early. Audrey at Farm all day.

Saturday 23
Got up fairly early. Didn't do much in morning. In afternoon, I did all the plain ironing while Mummy sewed. Eric Hillier came over for some mangoes. Dad and Merv went to cricket match in Goodna. Audrey went to Farm. Daisy and Maud (probably Yarrow) rode up to see me.

Sunday 24
Mr Dunhill and family came in morning and stayed all day. Mr D. tuned the piano. Lou Griffiths, Morgan, Meyrick, Leonie and Edie Martin came over in afternoon and played tennis. Morg., Leon and Edie stayed for tea. Mum drove Dunhills back to Goodna at night. (Mum would have been just 36 years old then.)

Monday 25
Mum and I slept or read all morning - until half-past twelve, when Daddy came back from Brisbane. He took Audrey back to school. Sickening to think of next Monday. Mum sewed all afternoon, and I read or played "Soldiers of the Queen" - I think it's something indescribably exquisite. We all went to bed pretty early. Am all on my lonely own now Audrey has gone to school.

Tuesday 26
Got up pretty early. A little after 10 Mum and I started to walk to Creek. Got out there long before the rest who rode - 4 of them, Aunties Audrey and Ivy, Maud and Daisy. Went for a walk a long way up O'possum Creek, where there were some lovely spots. Had a glorious time. Morgan drove Mum and me home as far as Farm. Lon Griffiths over at night.

Wednesday 27

Had breadfast in bed, but got up pretty early all the same.
Mummy sewed all day - made me a spotted blue dress. I
wasn't feeling at all well all day. I read most of the day or
had "Soldiers of the Queen". Had a lovely war dream last
night. Two fellows, Mr Reid and Mr Auld, were here for
dinner and part of the afternoon. Mr Lewis and son round
for orders. Janet Hardy and her sister were out for mangoes in afternoon. Jim Rice over to see Daddy for a little
while. Thelma Hillier came for honey. Ma over in afternoon with mail.

Thursday 28

Had breakfast in bed, but had work done early. Mummy
sewed again today - finished my dress and made a blouse
for herself etc. I went over to Farm in afternoon with the
mail. They made me stay to tea, so Merv (who was over to
dip) and I had tea there. Then all went down to dip -
nearly drowned a calf in the bargain. I came home after
eight with Auntie Audrey and Ivy. Heard that Ted P. was
engaged.

Friday 29

Worked really hard all day - that is, after 11 o'clock.
Before that Ivy and I drove to Goodna to catch the
mail and then waited for 9 o'clock mail. Stayed at
mill for a while, then went to station for fruit (which
wasn't there) then to Gibson's and then home. I wrote
to Chrissie in afternoon and sent Mr Hebden a birthday card. Getting very near school time again -
horrible.

Saturday 30

Got up very early and worked hard in morning. John
Hallett, Harold Woods and Willie Llewellyn were over
as Merv's guests, nearly all day. Mrs James and two
children over in afternoon, and stayed for tea. Got
two cases of fruit this morning. Mummy, Ma and I
drove to Labour meeting in school at night (Dad
rode).

Sunday 31

We all got up pretty late. Auntie Laura, Jim and Lollie over all day. Auntie Audrey and Ivy over in afternoon and also Morgan - we all chipped the tennis court, etc. Last day at home.

Monday 1

First day at school this year. Didn't like it so extra much. Ever so many new girls. One in my charge in our room. Had pretty fair lessons. Drove in with Mum this morning. Heard that Thelma (Tritton) wasn't coming back. Had a music lesson. Hate lessons now that the holidays have ended. Practised at 4.45pm.

Tuesday 2

Practised at 6.30. Then had a pretty fair day. Had a most tiring hour history lesson - never understood a thing Miss White was talking about. Read all the afternoon, or else talked. Nothing much doing yet. Not enjoying school very marvellously.

Wednesday 3

Practised at 6.30 again - horrible, as I was counting on study this morning. Had a very fair day. Liked every lesson - even Expansion for a wonder. Had a very nice algebra, and also a very nice geography lesson. New teacher Miss Hodgens was on duty. Week is passing very quickly. Haven't been home-sick yet, but would like to be home all the same. Got millions of lessons for tomorrow.

Thursday 4

Got up fairly early in order to learn lessons. Practised and had my music lesson in first prep. Had a nice day in spite of the most excruciatingly awful lessons. Had a nice German Grammar lesson. Also nice English hour lesson. Did some lessons after school this afternoon. Expected an awful history lesson, and had a lovely one. Got a lovely home letter this morning.

139

Friday 5

Had a very nice day. All lessons were nice. Mummy called for me early, and we drove straight home. When we got there (real early - half past five), I had a bonser feed of mangoes. Went to bed fairly early. Mummy called at Wilson's this afternoon for an explanation about Southport.

Saturday 6

Had breakfast in bed, but got up pretty early all the same. Had some visitors for mangoes in day time. In evening, Morgan and Meyrick came over and we played tennis. Jessie B. (?Brennan) and Kitty Mullins were over. Janet Hardy etc., were also out. A. Audrey and Ivy over at night.

Sunday 7

Got up pretty late. Intended going to Brennans' but Hansells came out in the car and Kerwicks came out also and took our physogues. A. Audrey, A. Laura and Ivy and Coralie over at night.

Monday 8

Drove in to school with Mummy in sulky but we were late as we had to distribute mangoes along the road. Had a very nice day. Nothing startling turned up. My parcel from Cribbs' has not turned up yet. I played a 31-game of tennis at a quarter past four with Jessie Coogan. Forgot to practise. Had a fair music lesson.

Tuesday 9

Got up to practise at 6.30, and found to my great satisfaction that I hadn't (to practise). Had a very nice day. Nearly went to sleep in history lesson. Then practised in first prep. this afternoon. The second should have had prep, but did algebra instead. But, best of all, it has been raining heavily all day. Read and did lessons this afternoon. Got parcel from Cribbs'.

Wednesday 10

Had a very nice day. Had real nice expansion. Had a middling music lesson. Then had pretty fair other lessons. Predictions of a great storm today or very soon. Stopped raining today, but everything still muddy. Got a letter from home this afternoon. Read "Pickwick Papers" until a quarter to five, then I played tennis with Muriel Collins and beat her 21-13, or something of the kind. Oh, well, goodnight. Don't know any lessons for tomorrow.

Thursday 11

Got up early and learnt lessons for today. Never so pressed for lessons before, I believe. Nevertheless got through the day nicely. Got a letter from Thelma this morning and she is coming up to our place for a weekend. Read all this afternoon and learnt a few English notes. Hilda (Withecombe) gave me a photo of herself and her father this evening. Nothing doing, so must wind up.

Friday 12

Had a fairly fair day (see it ??). Mummy drove in for me. Called for me about 3.30 and also drove Phyllis back to town with me. Saw Roy, but he wouldn't speak to us. We didn't do much in town, except go to Whitehouses'. Got home fairly early. Went to bed a little after nine. I played and sang (!) all the evening. I enjoyed it very much, thank you, but Mum and Merv didn't seem to appreciate it, somehow.

Saturday 13

Got up fairly early and worked like a Trojan until about 3 o'clock this afternoon. We put down new linoleum and put up new blinds etc. Allan Bourke arrived here per bike about 4 o'clock. Merv went to meet him on his bike. Morgan and Leonie came over in evening and we had a set of tennis. Had music, cards etc., at night.

Sunday 14

Had lots of visitors - mostly for mangoes. Morgan came over in afternoon, also Mat. Kerwin and Denis Kenny and we (A. Audrey, Ivy and I) and they played tennis. Smith's from Goodna, Crosses from Redbank, D. MacMahon also out.

Monday 15

Came back to school in sulky with Mummy and Auntie Laura - plus mangoes. Allan Bourke cycled home very early this morning. Had a frightful English exam. First lesson - didn't get it half finished as I was frightfully nervous. Had pretty good other lessons. Had a headache pretty well all day though. Played tennis this afternoon with Jessie Coogan and Muriel Collins. Broke, and got my badge mended.

Tuesday 16

Got up real early and felt horribly tired. Had fairly nice lessons. Miss Lilley got into one of her "little tempers" in English this morning. Then, Miss White asked questions in history for the first time - not extra bad. I got a letter from Thelma Graham this morning. Played a 31 game of tennis this afternoon with Jessie Coogan. Miss White's party for teachers, kids played up.

Wednesday 17

Got up early again. Went bowling down for my music lesson first prep. and found it changed. Had history exam., which would have been fairly nice, if there had been half enough time. It was raining in fits and starts all day. I got my German dictionary from home. Then I played tennis with Jessie Coogan, Muriel Collins and Margaret Gillies this afternoon. Practised this morning instead of this afternoon. Got millions of lessons to do tonight.

Thursday 18

Had a most frightful lesson day. Had geography exam. This afternoon. It was pretty fair, but I don't know my results yet. Got results of first history exam. from Miss White. I got 34 - I reckon it's good considering I hadn't nearly finished or looked over it. I had a nice music lesson this morning. I read for a while this afternoon and then practised. Got a letter from home.

142

Friday 19

Had a pretty fair day. But had German exam. this morning or afternoon or something. Also had arithmetic exam., following lesson. I have no results yet - perhaps, just as well. Drove home with Mummy. We went into town - Whitehouses, need I mention? - and got lots of things including a palm to decorate the sulky - eh?

Saturday 20

Got up fairly late. Then had breakfast and Mummy wrote letters. Ivors, Keith and Jimmy came over in morning. Oh! I forgot, I got up very late. Nothing doing in afternoon. But Ma came over and stayed for tea. I also did my lessons and read. I intended going to Farm at night, but we never went.

Sunday 21

Had over 30 visitors today, including Aunties Audrey and Ivy, Morg., Mey., Jessie, B. Mullins, J. Kenny, M. Kerwin, Crosses and lots of others. I went to Farm in morning and came back in afternoon.

Monday 22

Got up very early. Eating coconut ice all day. Mummy drove me in, and promised to get me some music. Got results of 3 exams. - geography - 47, German - 17, and arithmetic - 28. Not extra brilliant. I practised tennis for a while this afternoon with Jessie Coogan and Muriel Collins. Read and did lessons rest of time. Got "Prinzessin Ilse" tonight. So let it be.

Tuesday 23

Got up early and did some substantial work. Had a nice English lesson, i.e. for a "Shakespeare" one. Had a nice Arith. Lesson, only a lot of girls got into a row. Nearly went to sleep in history lesson. There was a very heavy thunderstorm for a little while this morning. All of us, i.e. V and VI forms, went for a long walk this afternoon by ourselves. Got a letter from Thelma.

Wednesday 24

Had a very nice day. Had the most awful Algebra exam. I ever even dreamt of or heard about, I got 13, and not lowest either. Got a letter from home, and one enclosed from Thelma in it. Got on real well in History. Played tennis this afternoon with Jessie Coogan and Muriel Collins. Hilda and I had a bit of a rat, but got over it now. Nothing else wonderful happened so must shut up. Oh, what can I do to fill up space - Puzzle.

Thursday 25

Got up real early. Had a fairly nice music lesson - short and sweet. Then had a very nice German lesson, but a pretty awful Algebra, on account of the awful marks we got for exam. Then had English exam. in hour lesson. I liked it and I think I ought to get more than I did last time. Had a lovely History lesson. We all got giggles. I got Thelma's book from box-room. Raining all the afternoon - hasn't stopped.

Friday 26

Had a very nice day. Came home by train this afternoon. Then I waited on station for Thelma. Thelma and Dad waited for Audrey and Ruth Dickson. Then we all drove home in the cart. We didn't do extra much at night. Thelma and I talked half the night and kept all the people awake. Ida was here. Uncle Dan also came up in afternoon. Nothing else.

Saturday 27

Thelma and I had breakfast in bed. In afternoon we had tennis match against Rices - and were beaten by 19 games. I played rottenly. But never mind, I got on spiffingly at night - had a glorious time. Danced and played games. Allan Bourke came out. Thelma went for a drive to Goodna.

Sunday 28

Got up first in house. Then in afternoon we played tennis as Morgan, Meyrick, Leonie and Edie Martin were over. Then at night, Morgan took Thelma and me for a heavenly drive in the moonlight. Zilpha Hillier's birthday party.

Monday 1

Thelma, Ida and I down to Goodna with Daddy this morning. Ida went by 7.20 train. I came up by 7.55 and Thelma by 8.15. Saw a couple of people and spoke to some of them, e.g. Jim Crookston, Jack Small, Harold Hillier, Morgan, etc. etc. Never did any lessons in week-end but got on alright today all the same. I can't possibly learn my English for tomorrow, so am looking forward to a good time.

Tuesday 2

Had a very nice day. It has passed awfully quickly. Had an abominable time in History lesson trying to keep awake. Have an awful lot of lessons to do this week. Looking forward to History exam. tomorrow. Couldn't play tennis this afternoon, as there were no spare courts. I read instead, and Jessie Coogan shared her chocolates. Nothing else wonderful happened.

Wednesday 3

Had a very nice day. The week seems to be passing awfully quickly, but don't know any lessons for tomorrow. Had 2nd History exam. today, and I got 38. Most of the girls got over 40. Got a letter from home this afternoon, also a telegram from Allan B.. Got an awful scare, when I saw it. Couldn't play tennis this afternoon, so did my German instead. A horrible dust storm started late yesterday, and hasn't gone down yet. We have been almost suffocated. Goodnight.

Thursday 4

Didn't know many lessons, but got on real well all the same. Miss White got real worked up in German and forgot the time, and went on another quarter-of-an-hour. Had a bonser time. So in consequence had a short English lesson. Then had a pretty bad Geography exam., then had a very nice History lesson. I got two letters this (morning), one a Prayer and the other from Thelma. Last tea tonight. Looking forward to tomorrow.

Friday 5
Had a fair day. Had two exams - arithmetic and German.
I got 22 for German - improving - I got 5 more than last
time. Daddy drove in for me and brought Mrs. O's honey.
Then we drove into town. I had ice cream and did some
shopping. Then we drove home and had biscuits, soft drinks
etc, on way home. Merv was away with Auntie Audrey and
the Red Cross doll. Then had a bit of music to myself at
night.

Saturday 6
Got up very late. Then Mum and I had to make up lost
time, and never stopped working all the afternoon. Then
at night, Daddy, Mummy and I drove over to Red Cross
social in the Hall. Had a ripping time. Had every dance
but one. Callaghan and Molloy played for all the dances -
bonser.

Sunday 7
Didn't get up until dinner time. Then in afternoon had lots
of people for mangoes and to visit us. Morgan, Meyrick, Ivy,
Tessie B., and Mr and Mrs and Mary B., other ones. Had
some tennis.

Monday 8
Drove in with Mummy in sulky. Were a bit later coming in
than usual, as had to dispose of a good many mangoes.
Had a very nice day. Had a pretty good music lesson. Then
had a fairly good German lesson. Got results of Arithmetic
examination. I got 41 - I reckon it's jolly good for me. Well
Mrs Hill has been round to put lights out, so good night.
Bought some chocolates.

Tuesday 9
Had a very nice English lesson, and I was looking forward
to an atrocious one. Then Marcie and Ida had a flare up
with Miss Carmody in Arithmetic lesson. Then had a very
nice sleepy History lesson. Played tennis with Jessie Coogan
this afternoon. Then for rest of time we talked to Girlie
Foote until teatime in 5th form. Had adventure in bath-
room with a spider.

Wednesday 10

Had a fair day. Had rather nice History lesson, and oh!
an indescribably atrocious algebra exam. - and Hilda
got 50! I got 21, and think that's jolly good. But I was
lowest. Then had a very nice Arithmetic lesson. This
afternoon as we couldn't play tennis, Jessie, Muriel and I
read and studied, and also ate a pineapple between us,
near the new courts - our usual haunt. Didn't get any
letters today. No more news. I do wish that this Wednesday space wasn't so big. We three went the round of all
the dorms this morning - had a lovely time. Three of us
devoured a pineapple.

Thursday 11

Didn't have a very extra nice music lesson. But had nice
algebra lesson. Then had a very nice German one, and
then had English Exam. in one hour lesson. Liked it all
right, only it was very long. Had questions in History this
afternoon - and although a lot of us did alright, Miss White
reckoned she wasn't at all pleased with it. Looked through
magazine and picture atlas with Dorothy McGill and
Marjorie Barnett until 4.45. Then practised until six. Got
my shoes. Got letter from home.

Friday 12

Had a fairly good day. Mummy drove in for me about 4
o'clock. She had been talking to Roy W. in town. We went
straight home. At least, Topper was awfully slow, so we only
got home about dark after gathering up all our belong-
ings. Practised at night and also got things together for
Brisbane tomorrow. I was last up tonight.

Saturday 13

Mum, Merv and I went to Brisbane this morning. Went to
the Doctor's and then out to Institution and got Audrey.
We all then went to Fegan's and as it was Audrey's birthday, we three kids had our physogues taken (See page 5). Then
we went for tramride to see place where I was born
(Enoggera Tce., Red Hill). Merv and I also went to Pictures, while Mum and Audrey went to Aunt Bess'. Saw
Eileen F. in town. Laurie Crowley came home with us.

Sunday 14

Got up pretty late. Ivy, Merv and I had game of tennis in morning. In afternoon, Wants and Coomb' were out. Also Farm people came over and stayed for a while at night. Mrs Harvey is very bad.

Monday 15

Got up extra early, as Mummy, Audrey and Laurie had to catch the 7.20 train. Was talking to Willie McKeon for a while on station. Had a pretty fair day. I forgot my music so in consequence had nearly all scales and arpeggios in my music lesson. I wrote home for it first thing this morning. Had a game of tennis with Jessie Coogan this afernoon, also read and studied (or pretended to).

Tuesday 16

Had a nice day. Practised what I could, as my music has not arrived yet. Had a nice History lesson. Expansion instead of Ransome. This afternoon watched the match between our girls and the boys from the Grammar. Bunny Dalton and Boy McCulloch were up, but didn't know me. Our girls lost by 54 points. Looking forward to History exam. tomorrow. Have done hardly any lessons.

Wednesday 17

Had a very nice day. Haven't got my music yet. It's getting serious. Had a most frightful History exam., but I managed to scrape up 35 for it. Had a very nice Algebra lesson. Then a nice Arith. one. I played tennis this afternoon with Jessie Coogan and Muriel Collins. Also shared their biscuits and toffee. Didn't get a home letter. Well, no more news, so must shut up. St. Patrick's Day, but per usual, we didn't get a holiday, or get to sports at Boy's Grammar. Cambrian concert tonight.

Thursday 18

Had a much nicer day than I expected to have. Had a very nice music lesson - short and sweet - as my music has not arrived from home yet. Had nice German and English lessons. Then had a very nice Geography exam., and a much nicer than expected Expansion lesson. Never got a home letter at all today. It's getting very serious. Looking forward to tomorrow afternoon.

148

Friday 19

Had a nice day. Had two exams running - German and Arithmetic. I came second for German. Vivian got 42 and then I got 28 - bit of a drop. Got Geography results. I came first with 46 marks. I drove home with Mum, much earlier than usual. Had a bit of music at night. Mum and I went down to see Mrs Harvey. The Tippets didn't turn up.

Saturday 20

Got up fairly early. Mum and I had a real day of it. Washed, ironed, did upstairs and hung up all new photos and pictures. Dad and Merv were away in Brisbane all day, and went to a Beekeepers' Meeting at night. Mum ironed at night, and I did my lessons until just before they came home.

Sunday 21

Got up at 3 minutes to 12. In afternoon, Mum and I went over to Farm. James' over there. Auntie Audrey at Harveys'. Willie McKeon, Morgan, Tom Martin and Victor Sutcliffe and a few people for mangoes - at our place. Mat. Kerwin, Auntie Audrey and Tom Waghorn over at night.

Monday 22

Got up very early. Drove down to Goodna in sulky with Daddy. Then came up with other girls in train. Had a nice day. Got results of Arithmetic Exam.: I got 26 (whole) marks. Had a short and sweet music lesson. I played tennis with Jessie Coogan this afternoon - we were quits. Then we talked rest of time - mostly about soldiers. Couldn't settle to any lessons tomorrow and am looking forward to English, as I forgot my Shakespeare.

Tuesday 23

Had a very fair day. Didn't pass very quickly though. Miss Lilley awfully nice when I told her about my Richard III. Had a real top notcha argument about "Fate", instead of History in hour lesson. Intended playing tennis this afternoon, but wrote to Audrey instead. Anniversary of Mum's Wedding Day. Had some cake from Muriel Collins this afternoon. Also finished my mangoes.

Wednesday 24
Got up pretty early. Had fairly nice day. Had Geography about same as usual - pretty disorderly. Then had a fairly nice Expansion lesson. I was very nearly asleep. Then had Algebra exam. - the last exam. this term. It wasn't very bad. I posted my letter to Audrey. Getting near the holidays now. Played tennis for a while with Jessie Coogan this afternoon. Also read some more of "Pickwick Papers". Never got home letter. Almost fainting to see the photos. Looking forward to all the lessons tomorrow. Girls played up a bit.

Thursday 25
Had a fairly nice day. Felt in an awfully bad humour this morning. Got on well in German and beautifully in English. We do nothing but read all the time in English now. Had a very nice History lesson. Got a letter from home this afternoon, but no photos have arrived yet - scandalous. Read and studied and practised this afternoon. This time next week will be home - bonz.

Friday 26
Had a very nice day. Drove home in trap with Mummy and got home much earlier than usual. Mummy went down to Harveys and stayed til after 11 o'clock, when Mrs. Honex died. Ivy came over for tea and I went back with her and stayed all night. We read etc., at night. I rode over to Farm from our place. Slept on verandah with Ivy.

Saturday 27
Came home very early. Mum washed and I cleaned 148 sides of panes of glass. Also practised for a good while. Mum ironed a bit at night, while I did my lessons. Dad and Merv drove to Goodna. Auntie Audrey was at Harveys' all day.

Sunday 28
Mrs Harvey was buried this morning. Mum went down to Harveys' and I went over to Farm in the morning. Jack Aspinall and Mr Thompson drove out this afternoon. House in an awful state.

Monday 29

Drove back to school much later than usual this morning. Had a very nice day all the same. Got on well with my lessons, although I didn't hardly any in the weekend. This afternoon, Wonder of WONDERS, I did some fancy-work!!!!!! We didn't play tennis, although we intended to. Nothing wonderful happened. I posted my letter to Thelma. Had a lot of cocoanut ice from Eileen. Also an apple from Hilda.

Tuesday 30

Had a very fair day. Got a beautiful letter from Thelma this morning. Had lovely English and History lessons, but pretty funny Arithmetic one. Had a very nice afternoon. Played tennis with Jessie this afternoon and won 21-16 or something. Had a bit of a hot bath, tonight instead of Jessie. Bit marvellous I finished my fancy work and washed it. Going to ask Jane to press it tomorrow.

Wednesday 31

Had a beautiful day. Had very nice lessons. Then, while I was supposed to be packing this afternoon, Eileen and I yarned and yarned. Then at 4.45, Hilda came up and the three of us visited V and VI dorms. But, most marvellous of all the delights, all the school had usual study, and then went out into the garden in the moonlight. Also, not by any means least, we all went over to the tuckshop and invested in lollies and fruit. Had a great feast on the turf in the moonlight. Feeling awfully excited.

Thursday 1

Last day of 1ˢᵗ term. We, i.e. V form, had a half holiday as we had made up our lessons before. I stayed at school until 3.30, when I went down town with Jessie and Muriel. Waited at Goodna for Mum and Audrey. Waiting with Dan in sulky, eating lollies. At night, Mrs Clyde, Miss Fletcher (sister) and Miss Ormerod arrived.

Friday 2

Working hard nearly all day. In morning Lou G., and Marshall Woods came over for game of tennis. I and visitors played for a while. In afternoon, Bowens, James, Morgan, Leonie and Doris Albury - Kerwicks - Jim and Sam Rice, Lou Llewellyn and George Dolan - were all over in the afternoon. Haven't had such a lot of visitors for a long time. Vera, Daisy and Priscilla Mossman were over for a good while.

Saturday 3

Merv and I and visitors played tennis and I learned to ride the bike spiffingly. Mrs Clyde drove to Goodna with Daddy. Sam Rice and Lou Llewellyn over in morning. All except Mum and me drove to scrub in afternoon. Marshall Woods, Auntie Audrey and Ivy were over.

Sunday 4

Dad took all the visitors for a ride in turns. Sam Rice, Lou Llewellyn, Meyrick, Mr Hertson, Con Nahrung, Mat, Keen, Alf Roberts, were all out during the day.

Monday 5

I went over to Farm in morning, and stayed until about 4 o'clock, when Auntie Audrey, Ivy and I walked to Goodna, went by train to Ipswich to the Eisteddfod. Had a real good time, but had also a lovely time coming home talking to soldiers in train (Forbes). Our visitors and the rest of us except me, all went for a picnic to Maller's Mountain. They got a carpet snake 12ft 6ins long and had a possum inside it. Auntie Audrey came home with me.

Tuesday 6

Auntie Audrey and I stayed in bed all day. We didn't intend to, but kept putting off getting up. Mum didn't intend washing either, but she did do it in the end. Auntie Audrey and I read nearly all day - magazines, and I read most of "Tom Brown's School Days". Auntie Audrey had a sleep in afternoon. Ivy rode over in evening. Had a lovely day.

Wednesday 7

Had a very easy day. Auntie Audrey went home early in morning with Dad, as he drove to Goodna to go by train to Board Meeting. Mum just fooled around and didn't do much besides damp down the clothes. I read nearly all day - best thing being "Little Eric Edgarton" - and in the afternoon tried to make cocoanut ice, and turned out cocoanut caramel. We all fell in love with it. Could ride the bike real well this afternoon. Went to bed early.

Thursday 8

Had breakfast in bed this morning. Mummy ironed nearly everything before dinner, while I washed up, did my room, unpicked my skirt etc.. This afternoon, none of us did much. I had some music and painting (!), reading and cutting out patriotic scraps etc.. Rode the bike real well this after-noon. Rode it down to corner of orchard. I simply adore it. Ma, Auntie Laura and Lollie were over this evening. Dad went down to Harveys.

Friday 9

Got up real early and went down to Goodna with Daddy to catch the mail. Talking to Aunt Eve. Muriel and Bridge arrived at mill last night from Southport. Mum at Farm when we got back. I stayed at Farm all day. They cleaned out the house, but I never did much but tidy out some draw-ers etc.. Stayed at the Farm all night.

Saturday 10

Went home real early in the morning. Merv and Dad caught the mail. In afternoon, Mum, Auntie Audrey, Ivy and I went to a picnic at Ferny Creek. Had a lovely time, and then went up to a scrumptious social in the Hall at night. We all walked up to Hall, and Mum drove and took refreshments etc.

Sunday 11

Gave Mummy her breakfast in bed, then neither of us got up until dinner time. Mum went over to Ben Josey's in after-noon. No visitors for a marvellous wonder. Bessie Josey's birthday.

Monday 12

Drove back to school with Mummy. Simply hated coming back after all the holidays - hated it more than ever before. Got on alright through the day. Had very nice lessons. Although I didn't practise in the holidays, I had a pretty fair music lesson. Played tennis on old courts this afternoon with Jessie C., Jean C., and Muriel C.. Also had glorious cake from Evelyn Horton. But, oh! Disappointment of disappointments, got a letter from Thelma T., saying she wasn't coming back.

Tuesday 13

Had a fair day. Didn't feel very happy though. I was cross, dissatisfied, headachy, tired and sleepy. Had a very nice English lesson, and also a very nice History lesson and disorderly Arithmetic. Teachers' meeting this afternoon. Had alright afternoon. Played tennis with Jessie Coogan, and won. Also read a lot of "Pickwick Papers". I was very pale today so I was informed, but felt alright.

Wednesday 14

Didn't have an extra nice day. Thought the lessons would never pass, but managed to get through alright. Had very nice lessons, all the same. Rained a bit at dinner time, and kept on pretty heavily all afternoon. Rain needed awfully badly everywhere. Read the everlasting "Pickwick Papers" this afternoon again. Got a letter from home this afternoon. No more so I must shut up. Got tons of lessons for tomorrow. I am beginning to hate lessons - too much of them.

Thursday 15

Had a very nice day. All our wing interviewed Mrs White this morning for making a row last night, but we got off scot free. Had nice lessons, especially German, English and History. No end of rows lately. I think there'll be an explosion soon. Boys from Grammar played our girls again this afternoon and won by 65 points. I nearly forgot to practise. Looking forward terribly to going home tomorrow.

Friday 16

Had alright day. Haven't started gymnastics yet. Go on well with all other lessons. Mummy called for me late - about quarter past four. We drove home together and picked up Mrs Hebden at Brennans'. She came up on Wednesday. Didn't do much at home. Went to bed pretty early in the stretcher in the sewing room.

Saturday 17

Did some work and made some cocoanut ice in morning. Merv, Dad and Ma went to Brisbane early and came home about three o'clock. In afternoon, Mum, Mrs Hebden and I went over to Farm. I went most of the way on the bike. Dad, Ivy and I drove and Auntie Audrey and Merv rode to Pictures and Dance in Hall.

Sunday 18

Stayed at Farm last night. Came home this morning with Ivors who stayed all day. In afternoon, Con Nahrum and J. Gibson came out, and Jim and Pam Rice and Lou Llewellyn also, Morgan. Mat. Kerwin over at night. Ivy over for a while.

Monday 19

Never learnt any lessons properly until I got to school. Had questions on notes in English, for a wonder. Got on very well in all other lessons. Was late in German, but Miss White didn't say a word. Muriel Collins and I were in Arbour until a quarter to five. I wrote a letter home thanking Mummy for the tin of chocolates I found in my basket. I did some German this afternoon. Miss Hill made me walk around for exercise this afternoon.

Tuesday 20

My birthday. Very important, as it only occurs once a year. Got darling little books from Chrissie and Miss Beetham. Also got post cards from Jessie Coogan and Allen B.. More than I expected. Had a very fair school day. Played tennis in afternoon with Jessie and Muriel. Also talking to Doris Foote for a good while. I posted a letter home this morning.

Wednesday 21

Had a very nice History lesson, but a rotten music lesson.
Got a post card for my birthday from Audrey this morning.
Got on alright in all other lessons too. Never got any mail
this afternoon. And on top of that, at a quarter to five, had
a most awful atrocious, horrible frightful, ghastly game of
basketball. It was indescribable. Got most awful lot of
lessons for tomorrow. Did some lessons this afternoon.
Excuse mistakes, as I am playing bo-peep with a blind.

Thursday 22

Had a nice Practice. Then had very nice Algebra. Pretty fair
German and then First English Exam. this term. It wasn't too
bad, but goodness me, I will be glad if I get a decent mark at
all. Learnt History with Edna Hadley at Dinner Time. Miss
Carmody and Dorothy McGill had a big row in Geography.
Had a lovely History lesson. Got a home letter this afternoon.
Felt awfully "dumpy" several times today.

Friday 23

Had very nice lessons. Wasn't very well in the morning.
Had real nice Gymnastic lesson. Dad rang up Mrs O. and
said that I had to come by train. It rained in afternoon,
but I got down to station dry and had talk to station
master. Arrived in Goodna by 5.45 train, where I drove
home with Ma and Auntie Audrey. Con Nahrung, Miss
Taylor and Audrey were there when I arrived.

Saturday 24

Auntie Audrey stayed all night last night, so we stayed in
bed this morning. I had a dose of castor oil - lovely. Felt
pretty bad all day. Miss Taylor went driving with Dad in
morning and afternoon. Audrey over at Farm in morning. Auntie Laura, Ma and Lollie came over in evening. I
wrote letters to Thelma T., and Chrissie.

Sunday 25

Got up late again. Smith's out in afternoon. Audrey and I
went for a heavenly drive with Morgan all round Asylum
and up to Redbank and back. Did some lessons. Made some
jelly and cocoanut ice.

Monday 26
Drove down with Daddy, Miss Taylor and Audrey. They
went down by 7.20 train with Con Nahrung. Merv stayed
on station with me until train time. Forgot my music, so
had to write home. Think I saw Mr Mick Molloy at E.
Ipswich this morning. Had very nice lessons. Wasn't feeling
extra fit all day. Had a game of tennis this afternoon with
Jessie Coogan. Talked rest of time. Had some lollies and
fruit.

Tuesday 27
Had an alright day, and felt a little better than
yesterday. Had a silly History lesson, Marcie got into a
row for not knowing some French. Had alright other
lessons. Dorothy McGill and Marjorie Barnett came to
visit us upstairs. Did a bit of Geography this afternoon.
Had a good talk to Girlie and Marjorie Foote. Lost
two lead pencils, so am nigh stony broke. Hope the
week will pass quickly.

Wednesday 28
Had very fair day - but only fair. Had Geography Exam..
It wasn't too bad. Then had a fair History lesson, and on
top of that had Algebra Exam.. It was awful. I felt like
howling, but managed to scrape up 21 marks. Had a pretty
nice music lesson. Best of all, which bucked me up, Ivy came
up to see me before school, and also brought my music and
a letter from home. Had a game of basket ball and wonder
of wonders, I liked it a bit. Nothing else. Kept in tonight in
study for laughing.

Thursday 29
Had a very nice Algebra lesson. Then I didn't know
anything in German, and Miss White did a good bit of
chucking off in consequence. Had a very nice English
lesson, Miss Lilley in a pretty good mood, for about the
first time since last week. Very nice Geography Exam..
Then rather nice History - started pretty bad, but
ended up beautifully. Did some lessons and played
tennis this afternoon. Miss Lilley lectured some of us in
the form room.

Friday 30

Had a very nice day, and got on well in all the lessons I had. Dying to get home. I went half way into Ipswich with Jessie Coogan and got caught in the rain. Came back and found my basket was gone, but managed to get it back. Mummy called for me about twenty past four and we had a bonser drive home, as it was nearly dark.

Saturday 1

Got up fairly early. Didn't do extra much. Dad drove down after dinner for Myfanwy (Parry) and then about four o'clock, Ted Palmer arrived on his bike. We had some tennis, and at night Aunties Laura and Audrey and Ivy and Coralie came over and we had a musical evening.

Sunday 2

George Allen and Allan Bourke came out on bikes early. Raining nearly all day, so we sang hymns while it was on, and played tennis when it was fine. Aunties Audrey and Ivy over at night.

Monday 3

Two boys went home awfully early, but George A. stayed. Then Dad drove Vonnie and me down to Goodna, and came up by train. Had a very nice day. Got some chocolates this morning. Been raining a good deal all day. Jessie took me down to East Ipswich this afternoon for a parcel, where we waited to see 5.20 train. Miss White took some of the girls for a walk. Frightful music lesson.

Tuesday 4

Got on fairly alright in English, though my analysis was all wrong. Then had a very nice History lesson, not so sleepy as usual. Had a very nice practise, finding out meanwhile that Ida Adcock knew Cecil Robinson. Raining nearly all day again. Jessie shared a pineapple after school. I did the cutting and also a share of the eating. Hilda hasn't arrived yet. Feeling crazy about "day girl" business after Middy.

Wednesday 5

Had a very fair day. Had History Exam in Hour instead of third lesson. I didn't like it extra much, and then on top of that, we had the most cruel, Arithmetic Exam.. Been sprinkling rain a little now and then today, but not much to speak of. Shared some more of Jessie's birthday cake this afternoon. Taking to Girlie Foote for a while. Heard there is a big casualty list of Queenslanders today, but haven't seen it yet. Only know that the Rev. Robertson's son was killed in action. Dreadful. I feel as if I'd like to howl, which I will do if anyone I know is killed.

Thursday 6

Terribly long list of deaths today, 2 Ipswich men - Robertson and Roberts among them. Had very nice practise and Algebra lesson. Then had a much nicer German lesson than usual and a same English lesson. Then had awfully nice Geography and History lessons. Mrs O. had something on this afternoon for the Belgiums, but, of course, we weren't in it. Held meeting at dinnertime about Bazaar.

Friday 7

Had a very fair day. Had German Exam. and managed to get 31. Not too bad, I think it is the highest I have ever got. Drove home with Mummy in sulky. Topper was frightfully knocked up so even though I walked up some of the hills, we got home very late. Merv and I stayed up until 10.30pm. I was playing (piano) and Merv was reading. Edith Winlaw left school.

Saturday 8

Got up at nine. Mum and I did hardly any work in the morning. Mum was trying to make my blouse, but in the afternoon, both of us took it over to Farm for Auntie Audrey to finish. I rode bike over, and stayed all night. Did my lessons at night. Pictures in hall at night, but none of us went.

Sunday 9

Came home in morning and sorted music, etc. Will Rice came over for game of tennis. Jim Rice also over. Con Nahrung over all afternoon. Also all Farm people in evening. Mat Kerwin over at night.

Monday 10

Drove down to Goodna with Dad and Merv. Then came up by train and had a very nice day. Got on well in all lessons, pretty fair in music lesson. This afternoon Jessie and I had to mend a net on the new tennis courts, but we haven't finished it yet. Miss Hill is putting lights out, so must shut up. Looking forward to English Exam..

Tuesday 11

Posted card to Vera for her birthday. Had a very nice day but a most horribly frightfully sleepy History lesson. Also had very nice English Exam., only I didn't have time to finish it. Jessie and I finished the net this afternoon. I did some knitting, also talking to Mary Foote for a time. Miss White is on duty tonight, and took us for study, so must hurry up and get into bed. Frightfully sleepy, and got oceans of lessons for tomorrow.

Wednesday 12

Had a very nice day. Only marred by having a terrible Algebra exam., but managed to scrape up 21 marks. Then had a most awful beginning to Arithmetic lesson, but don't know how it will end. Had a glorious music lesson as Miss Cadogan told me all about Germany and its customs nearly all the time. Then this afternoon played basketball and went a whopper on the ground. But, most glorious of all, Auntie Audrey and Ivy came up to see about half past five. Ivy is getting her certificate. They brought me some chocolates and bananas.

Thursday 13

Had a very nice practice and Algebra lesson. Then had a good German one, and the most glorious English lesson I have had this year, I think. But had a row with Eileen this morning about towel rack. Finished my chocolates and bananas today. Ethel Nicol's Birthday also. Then had alright Geography and History lessons. Miss Woods made us play tennis this afternoon. Then I read rest of time. Didn't get a home letter.

Friday 14

Had a very nice day. Got a letter from Mum this morning, saying that I could meet in town, but as it looked very rainified this afternoon, I didn't go. So Mum called up at Grammar for me about half past four. It rained a little going home. Got home just after dark. I wasn't at all well, but got alright after tea, and had some music.

Saturday 15

Had a pretty bad cold, so didn't get up until all hours. Mum just fooled round all morning. Ma came over for dinner. Dad and Merv went to Goodna in morning. It rained hard nearly all afternoon. I had some music and painting and also did a lot of knitting for soldiers. Wrote to Audrey and Miss Beetham.

Sunday 16

Got up about nine. Dad and Merv went down to inspect waterhole, so Mum and I took dinner down and had it there. For a wonder, no one came in afternoon, so I did a lot of lessons. Aunties Audrey and Ivy over at night.

Monday 17

Came back to school by train. Drove as far as Goodna with Daddy and Merv. It was - well - er - er - atrociously cold getting up. I nearly expired (!). Had an alright day of lessons. Then played tennis for a while this afternoon with Jessie C., and then we went down to Muriel in the Arbour. Got tons of lessons for tomorrow. Saw one of the Colemans on Bundamba station and Mr Molloy on East Ipswich this morning. Nothing else turned up. Awfully nice music lesson.

Tuesday 18

Read some of the "Blue Bird" this morning. I love it so far. Had very nice lessons. Alright English and pretty good Arithmetic and Algebra. Miss White went over our "uniform" marks in History, but the History was awfully interesting. Viv got an impos. in Latin this afternoon, which is dreadful. Talking to two Footes this afternoon. Pretty cold, at least that's how I feel. Miss Cadogan going to read her paper on "Music" at St. David's thing-me-bob. At least I thought so, but wrong.

Wednesday 19

Had a very short and pretty sweet music lesson. Then alright other lessons. But had an excruciatingly awful History Exam., and an alright Arith one, but I couldn't do much. It was cold and windy again today. I nearly "fruz". Talked to Edna Hadley in playshed this afternoon until a quarter to five, when I had to play basket ball and as a matter of course, or in other words, make a fool of myself. Looking forward to a great day tomorrow of lessons. Got nothing else to say. Hilda and Eileen are at daggers, so I must try to clear up things if possible.

Thursday 20

Lovely (!) cold morning and I had a great struggle to get into an icy bath. Had very nice German lesson, but best English lesson for ages. Had it out in the Garden. Then had very nice Geography lesson and went over history Exam. in History lesson. Talked to Hilda first and afterwards Eileen this afternoon. I got 35 for history. No one got as high marks as last time though. Got frightfully sore hands. I suppose with the wind and rubbing them to keep warm.

Friday 21

Had very alright lesson day. Had German Exam. and scraped up 29 marks. Got a letter from home this morning saying to go home in 5.20 train, but Dad rang up and said to go in 4.10, so went by that. Met Merv in Goodna and got some lollies from Gilsons, and then drove home with Dad. Mr Digby Denham drove Miss Shepherd and Audrey up from Brisbane to Goodna and Dad drove them home from Goodna after the meeting.

Saturday 22

Audrey and I got up very late - after ten, I think. Dad over at polling booth all day. Mum also went over to vote. Merv went to Goodna in morning. Heard that Joe Coogan was wounded at Dardanelles. Audrey and I went to Farm and came home with Auntie Audrey and Ivy at night. Got my coat and skirt fixed up.

Sunday 23

Got up fairly early. Went over to Farm on bike. Dad and Merv drove to Josey's and Audrey as far as Farm in morning. In afternoon, Ron. Nahrung, Mr Warner, Cane, Falby, Gibson, Morgan and Meyrick played tennis. Mat. Kerwin over at night. Auntie Audrey and Ivy over too.

Monday 24

Came down in sulky to Goodna with Daddy, Miss Shepherd and Audrey. Just caught the train and then I found I'd forgotten to get any money. So cut across to the mill and got some from Daddy. Had an alright day of lessons. Talked to Edna Hadley in playshed for good while this afternoon and then went into Arbour with Jessie and Muriel. My hands are again a bit sore. Trying to listen to Eileen singing, so my writing is a failure.

Tuesday 25

Not so extra cold this morning, but had enough all the same. Had Arithmetic lesson out in the Garden. Then had just-as-usual Algebra, English and History lessons. This afternoon Jessie rang up and took me with her - great sport. Then we played tennis for a little while, and then went down into Arbour and Jessie knitted while I talked. The week isn't going quickly enough for my liking.

Wednesday 26

Had part of Geography out in the Garden. Had very nice History lesson, and then had another atrocious Algebra Exam.. Don't know what will become of mine. Got a home letter about the show this morning. Got on well in Arithmetic, only Hilda and Ethel were sent to office. They were with Miss White all afternoon, etc.. I played in a monthly match this afternoon but lost. Then I went down to Arbour and talked to Jessie, then did some English and then talked to Eileen. Looking forward to tomorrow.

Thursday 27

Got on well in all lessons this morning. Then after dinner walked down town then took a car out to Show grounds where I met Daddy and Aunties Laura and Audrey. Looked at the Ring nearly all afternoon. After some refreshments, we had a walk through the building, then the sideshows and then back to the Grandstand. Didn't see extra many people that I knew. Drove back to school before tea. Studied a bit tonight, and read and danced rest of the time.

Friday 28

Got on nicely at school. Came home by train and met Daddy at Goodna and drove straight home. Ivors and Audrey were over there and stayed all night, so that they can stay with me tomorrow. Put kiddies to bed after tea and then had some music to entertain myself until pretty late. Miss Woods got news of her brother's death. Pretty cold today.

Saturday 29

Got up early as Mummy went to Bris. with Miss Harvey and Leila Stephens. They saw the procession too. About 3,000 volunteers marched right through Brisbane. It was awfully sad, I believe. Ivors and Audrey stayed with me all day, until Auntie Laura and Ivy came over at night for them. Merv went to footbball match at Redbank and won 3 or 4 - 1.

Sunday 30

Got up late. Did my lessons this afternoon, and had no visitors, which is something very unusual. At night, Mum, Merv and I from here, and Aunties Audrey, Laura and Ivy, and Ivors and Audrey from Farm went over to Anniversary at the Church.

Monday 31

Got up very early and drove down to Goodna with Dad and Merv and came up to school by train. Had alright English and other lessons. But had an atrociously dreadful music lesson - couln't play a thing. Had practice and German mixed up this afternoon as Miss White went down town early. Therefore we had half an hour prep.. Got an invitation to dance from Allen B. this afternoon, but don't think I will go. Read Boys' Grammar mag., and talked this afternoon and evening.

Tuesday 1
Had very nice Arithmetic and Algebra lessons. Then Zoe Martin took us for dumb-bells, as Miss Woods is away, so didn't do much but fool. Then had English in garden, then pretty good History lesson. Did some Geography in dinner hour with Edna Hadley. Speaking to Doris Foote for a while this afternoon, and read, and played tennis with Jessie C., and Jean Cramond this afternoon.

Wednesday 2
Pretty cold again this morning. Had a very nice music lesson. Miss Cadogan was in a bonser mood. Had geography Exam. this morning. I liked it pretty well. Then had a lovely History lesson, and also a nice Algebra one. Saw that W. H. Rea from Victoria was wounded at Dardanelles. Over 300 Victorians were killed in this morning's paper. Terrible now. Very nice lessons in afternoon. Read then until a quarter to five, and then had the funniest game of basket ball I ever had or saw. I could do hardly anything but laugh.

Thursday 3
The only holiday in the year so made the most of it. About 10am V and VI walked out to Kholo (6 miles away) with Miss Cribb. Rode part of the way on a bullock waggon. Paddled, etc., out there, and had one of the most ripping times I have ever had. The rest of the Lower School went for a motor-boat picnic this afternoon with Miss White. Eileen and I had an exciting comedy on the lawn tonight. Waited on ourselves at tea and also washed up. Came to bed early.

Friday 4
Had Arithmetic and English Exams.. Neither of them were too bad, but I didn't finish my English. Mum met me at school about half past four. We drove slowly home. Merv has been in bed since Wednesday with influenza. Still pretty bad tonight. Not having any music tonight, as am going straight to bed. My legs awfully stiff. Tom Coogan's reported wounded.

Saturday 5

Never got up until nearly dinner time. Auntie Audrey and Ivy were over in the morning. They went to Ferny Creek Picnic and Dance and had a glorious time. Mum and I worked hard all the afternoon. Daddy went to a Beekeeper's meeting in Brisbane at night. Merv is still in bed, but better than before. I had some music at night, while Mum did some cooking.

Sunday 6

Got up early. Ivors and Audrey over in morning. Merv stayed in bed all day, but nothing much wrong with him except a cough. I went over to Farm in morning to hear about the Picnic and Dance. Ivy and Tom called up in afternoon.

Monday 7

Drove down to Goodna with Daddy in sulky with Larry. Came up by train and heard all about the Tennis match at the Glennie. Had an alright English and a very nice music lesson. After which Miss Cadogan played me two pieces which she is going to play at Allies' Fete. Did my Essay in the Arbour nearly all the afternoon, and then read in V. Form from 5.15pm. until the dressing room. Am in a hurry, so goodnight.

Tuesday 8

Had a very nice day. Got on well in all the lessons. Nice History lesson and practise, but only talked to Dorothy McGill in last prep. It rained a good deal this after-noon, and there was a fairly heavy storm, but has cleared up a bit now. Did some lessons and read all this afternoon. Jessie C. made me a golliwog, which I now have round my neck. Got a letter from Thelma Tritton this morning. Jessie made me a golliwog.

Wednesday 9

Most frightfully cold this morning, and I nearly froze all morning. Had a very nice music lesson, and we all apologised to Miss Cribb this morning for misbehaviour in class. Hadn't such a nice History lesson as usual. Wore my golliwog for first time today. Most bitterly cold wind blowing this afternoon. I studied until a quarter to five, when I had to play basket ball. I played better than I have ever done before (but that doesn't flatter me at all). Got a bit of headache since and feel feverish. I'm sure I'm done for.

Thursday 10

Had a very nice morning, although I think it was colder than it has ever been this winter. At least, that's what I think. Had a pretty awful German lesson and a glorious English one. We went over Exam., by the way, I only got 32 for Exam.. Has a most atrocious History Exam. this afternoon. I simply hated it. Then did German in the Arbour until a quarter past five, and then read until the dressing bell. Felt most frightful all day. No home letter.

Friday 11

Got on well in lessons all day. Got a home letter this morning. I went home by 20 past 5 train, and in consequence got some German ahead, especially as I was excused from Gymnastics. Met Dad in Goodna, and we waited on platform until Miss Taylor and Audrey arrived, when we all drove home together. A QT. reporter, Mr Simpson, stayed the night here.

Saturday 12

Audrey and I had breakfast in bed and got up very late. Miss Taylor drove to Goodna with Dad in morning and Audrey went as far as Farm with them. Merv went to his football match, Goodna v Redbank, in afternoon and won. We all went up to the Bees, where we had a picnic and bonfire. Mr Chappell arrived this evening and stayed all night. Campbell's over at night. Heard that George Pettinger was killed in Dardanelles.

Sunday 13

Got up late. Mr and Mrs and Russell family here in afternoon. Mr Hillier called. Mum drove Miss Taylor and Audrey to meeting at Ryan's. I went over to Farm, and brought Auntie Audrey and Ivy back with me, and had a game of tennis, and music at night.

Monday 14

Had a great rush to catch the 20 past 7 train. I had to help Miss Taylor and Audrey and then go back for my basket, etc.. Came up by 5 to 8 train, and had a pretty good day. Miss Lilley wasn't in an extra good temper, and kept most of the class in. Had a very nice German lesson. Read and talked most of afternoon and I played tennis with Jessie for a while too. Lights supposed to be out, so must shut up. Just had a banana. Jessie rang up Rosewood.

Tuesday 15

Got on well all day. Couldn't find my "Quentin Durward", but Miss Lilley was very nice about it. Got on well in History too. Miss White went over our Exam., I shone out with 31 marks. Read and then played tennis for a while this afternoon with Jessie C., Phyllis Cos., and Evelyn H.. Finished "Pickwick Papers" this evening. Big bust up between V and VI dorms this end. Miss White came on the scene and V dorm had to do study for an hour extra in VI form.

Wednesday 16

Got in a pretty big bit of a temper first thing this morning, but kept it to myself, and have forgiven the girls and quite got over it now. Got on beautifully in my Music lesson. Talked nearly all the time, and therefore didn't get through my pieces. Got on well also in History lesson. Read "The Haunted Man" by Dickens this afternoon. Then I had a very nice game of basket ball. Then read some more of my book until dressing bell. Miss White is going to be on duty every evening from this until the end of the term. Eileen and I went down and heard Miss Cadogan playing some glorious pieces before study.

Thursday 17

Had an alright nice day. Not so cold these days. Got on well in English and German. Then studied History with Edna Hadley at dinner time. Had very nice geography lesson, but Miss White told me in History to please not study that of America so hard, or I was sure to get brain fever. Wish she meant it. As it happened though, I wasn't really the one to blame. But 2 minutes afterwards Mum came to see me, so greatly compensated for it. Played tennis with Jessie, and read, and swang with Eileen this afternoon.

Friday 18

Had a very nice day. Had the worst German Exam. I ever had but managed to get 29 marks. Wonder of wonders! Had alright other lessons. Went home by ten past four train to Goodna all on my lonely-own. Met Merv on station, and we went down and bought lollies, then Mum came and we all drove home together. Mum and I stayed at Farm until 10 o'clock, fixing dresses. Then walked home. Great preparations at school today for Allies Market tomorrow.

Saturday 19

Got up pretty late. Mr Reid landed home from Goodna with Merv this morning, and stayed until after dinner. Mum went over to Farm this afternoon, and I fooled about at home. Then when we were all ready to go to Kitty Mullins' presentation, a terrific storm came on and silky oak was struck in the orchard. Then went to Hall and had a glorious time. Allies Market on at school.

Sunday 20

Didn't wake until Mummy woke me at half past ten. Got up soon after, and didn't do much all day. In afternoon Mr and Mrs Smith and Maggie Keene drove out from Goodna. Mum and I had some music tonight, and came to bed early.

Monday 21

Drove down to Goodna with Dad and Merv. Had experience with Price's cousin in train. He must have felt flattered, from my knowing him by his red head. Had to stay in for my poetry for Miss Lilley, but shouldn't have had to. Got on well in other lessons. I was just told that Phyllis spoke to me today but I didn't hear her, so I suppose she's offended. Got magazines at dinnertime, but they're rotten. V had early time table today. Had a glorious music lesson. Miss C. told me all about Saturday.

Tuesday 22

It was very cold this morning. I nearly froze in the bath. Got on well in all lessons. Had alright English, but a frightfully sleepy History lesson. Don't think I can possibly wait for the holidays, as 3 whole days yet. Played tennis with Jessie and Muriel this evening. Had neuralgia nearly all day and felt queer this afternoon (s'pose nothing to what I looked) Oh shut up! I'm getting frivolous or sleepy or something.

Wednesday 23

Wasn't quite as cold as usual. Had a very nice music lesson. Last one I ever have here, I hope. Also had fairly nice History lesson and then an alright Algebra one. Miss Carmody read to us out of Scribner's Mag. about New Canadian Railway, all Geography lesson. Got on alright this afternoon. No Tennis at all this afternoon, so Eileen and I sat near old Tennis courts and first of all did German and then I read out "The Battle of Life" to Eileen, while she knitted. Had some tickling on the floor after as well, and nearly went mad. Glad the week is half over.

Thursday 24

Got two letters from home this morning and afternoon. Hardly any extra lessons to do today. Got on well in all lessons. Never did a bit of practising this morning. Jessie, Ida Adcock and I talked instead in music rooms. Packed this afternoon and then finished reading out "The Battle of Life" to Eileen. Have a pretty stuffy cold tonight, so have taken an aspirin. My hands are also awfully chapped and sore. Looking forward to tomorrow.

Friday 25
Got on alright with lessons, but Miss Lilley in a bit of a rat in English this afternoon. Dad drove in for me a little after 4.30pm, and we went home with Mrs. G's hat boxes, and broke five good panes of glass. Don't think I ever enjoyed (!!!) a drive so much. We all walked over to Hillier's at night, in order to arrange some of our concert programme. Awfully cold and blowing, but gloriously moonlight. My cold is pretty bad - worse than yesterday.

Saturday 26
Audrey and I got up late. This is first day of Mid-winter Holidays. This afternoon the kids came to practise singing for concert and we also read our dialogue through a few times. Mummy has already sold a few of Mrs O's saleables. Nothing else much happened. Didn't do anything special, so goodnight.

Sunday 27
My cold pretty bad in afternoon, Mr and Miss Kerwick and Mr Irquett (!) drove out. Dad and Mr Kerwick tried to shoot some turkeys, but failed. Mat. Kerwin and Auntie Ivy and Audrey over at night.

Monday 28
First real day of holidays. Got up late. Auntie Audrey and Ivy brought washing over from Farm. Auntie Audrey sewed for us all day while Mummy and Ivy washed. I did nearly all the housework and also some sewing. At night although we weren't keen on it we all (except Dad) from here, went over to the Band of Hope. It was very much nicer than usual. Audrey recited. Evelyn Hallett objected to being in the dialogue. Aunt Eve over in evening.

Tuesday 29
I rode over to Farm on bike in the morning, and arranged a bit more about our dialogue. Holidays not passing any too slowly. In afternoon kids came to practise singing for concert, and at night, we had dialogue rehearsal. Leonie (Jones)and Edie Martin came to see me in the afternoon. I like Edie very much. Leonie and Evie Hillier took parts in the dialogue. Mr Nash killed at Dardanelles.

Wednesday 30

Ivy and Auntie Audrey called up in morning, and I went home with them and stayed all day. Dad drove Mummy to Goodna about dinner time, where she caught the train to Ipswich. Audrey and Merv came as far as Farm with them, and stayed there. I took a flying trip home with Ivors and Audrey B. in afternoon. Dad called for Auntie Audrey and me about 6.30pm and we drove down to Goodna, where we met Mum at mill. Then all went to Oddfellow's Hall to the Farewell Social to Goodna volunteers, George Gibson, Mundy, Mayes, Hehr etc.. Had a lovely time. Other soldiers were there, and especially Moynahan (Sergeant) who had "(eyes)".

Thursday 1

Got up fairly early. Mum, Merv and I made marmalade jam all the morning. Giff. Evans was here for orders in morning. Audrey came home with Farm people in afternoon. Then all of us from here, and Auntie Audrey, Ivy, Ivors, Audrey and Tom from Farm, went up to the "Bees" and pulled nearly all the old house down. Auntie Audrey came up here for tea and went home afterwards. I did a bit of ironing at night. Feeling dead tired.

Friday 2

It was rainy in the morning. Kiddies came over to rehearsal in afternoon, and also dialogue people - most of these also practised at night. Should have gone out to Creek tonight, but was a little damp and as Leonie and Edie were riding we didn't go. Haven't written any letters yet, but just can't be bothered, although am awfully worried about it.

Saturday 3

Got up pretty late. About 10.30am. Audrey, Merv and I went out to O'possum Creek. Merv came home in afternoon, but Audrey and I stayed all night. In afternoon, Edie Martin, Leonie, Audrey, Merv, Jack and I went for a walk up the Creek. At night had riddles etc., and then all of us girls slept in the one bed. Had a great time.

Sunday 4

Got up very late. Played rounders etc. in afternoon. Morgan drove Audrey and me home at night. Leonie and Edie walked over and then drove home with Morgan. Mat Kerwin called at night.

Monday 5

Aunties Audrey and Laura and Ivy brought washing over. Auntie Audrey sewed all day. I did nearly all housework and helped a bit with washing. In evening, helped carry washing down to corner, and then we all had a great time trying to catch Secret., as Ivy and Tom came over to catch him too. Ma sent for the doctor to come to Eva Waghorn as she is pretty bad

Tuesday 6

Got up late. Mum ironed in morning. In afternoon Mum and Audrey went out visiting in the village and I spent the time at the Farm. Rode home with Merv. Marshall Woods came over at night, and we had a great go in about the war. Dr McEvoy came out early to see Eva, and sent for ambulance, who came out and took her to General Hospital this afternoon. She has double pneumonia.

Wednesday 7

Audrey and I got up pretty late. Mum did a lot of sewing, and then in the afternoon, the dialogue girls came over, and we had a bonser rehearsal. We, i.e., nearly all of us, got blackened up and also dressed in dialogue things, just to get used to it. It was great fun. Ma came over and listened to the rehearsal. Audrey Barns and Evie Hillier came this way from school. Nothing else very wonderful happened. I do "hope and trust" that next Diary I get won't have such a long Wednesday in it, as I can not possibly get it filled up with anything but rot.

Thursday 8

Mummy sewed and packed Audrey's basket nearly all day, while Audrey and I did nearly all the housework. In the afternoon, dialogue girls came over for another rehearsal. We are getting much better. Auntie Laura, Ivy and Coralie came over to watch us. It was raining a bit in the morning, also a little in the evening, but everyone came but Annie Smith. Marshall Woods should have been over tonight, but didn't turn up.

Friday 9

Got up pretty late. Then had early dinner, and we
(Mummy, Audrey and me; Auntie Audrey, Zilpha and
Thelma) went over to decorate the Hall for the concert
tomorrow night. Had a lovely time. Kiddies came up after
school and practised their songs, and we had several
rehearsals, and landed home after dark. Hall looks lovely.
Ivy went to Bris. to apply for position at Infants' Home, but
was too late.

Saturday 10

Washed our heads and fooled round all day until about 4
o'clock when we started getting dressed for concert (in aid
of Wounded Soldiers). I got blackened and dressed for "Girl
Serenaders" before I left. Concert a great success. Had a
glorious time. We (all) stayed black for the dance, and
had a bonz. time.

Sunday 11

All got up very late and very tired. In afternoon Mum,
Auntie Audrey and Zilpha Hillier went over and cleared up
the Hall. Audrey and I went over to Farm and spent the
afternoon there.

Monday 12

Got up very early this morning, as Audrey went back to school.
Ma took her down and also did some shopping for me. Mum
and I intended going but didn't. I wrote four letters in the
morning, and arranged postcards in the Album in afternoon.
Got a paper with Major A. W. Nash's death in it. I got a second
letter from Jessie explaining affairs. Had some music at night,
and helped Merv with his lessons.

Tuesday 13

Got up fairly early. Mum and I washed, and also did some
extra homework this morning. Ivy called up to see us this
afternoon and brought us some cakes (which didn't last
long), and we all had a great laugh over the concert.
Mat. Kerwin came over at night, also Auntie Audrey and
Ivy and we fixed up the proceeds of concert, which
amounted to   £10-0-2 (great).

Wednesday 14

I didn't get up until all hours and as Mum was in bed sick all morning, there was not very much done. Then soon after dinner we went over to Farm to get Mum's navy blue dress altered. We stayed until dusk, then came home, and Mum pulled up water, while I brought down the cows. Dad was away at a motor boat trip all day, and didn't arrive home until we did. Oh, dash it and darn it and hang it all!!!! I wish this wasn't so long, as nothing at all wonderful ever happens to me to write down here.

Thursday 15

Had a great go in at the kitchen today. I cleaned silver and things, while Mummy cleaned the stove and white-washed, etc.. Then about 3 o'clock Leonie came up to pay Mummy for the things from Allies' Market. So I talked to her for about an hour and a half about concert, etc.. Holidays nearly over. It is sickening to think of it. Goodnight, und Guten Nacht. Walked down for the butter.

Friday 16

Intended doing a lot of work, but only finished doing the kitchen thoroughly. Dad drove down to Goodna for Pa (who arrived from Charleville) this morning. So about 4 o'clock Mum and I walked over to the Farm to see Pa and didn't return until pretty late. Had tea over there. Arranged to go down to Brisbane with Ivy tomorrow morning. So fixed up my vacation form, etc. Nothing else to fill up space.

Saturday 17

Got up awfully early. Then drove to Goodna with Dad and went down to Bris. by 8.15 train (with Ivy). Went to dentist's, pictures, Uncle Dan's Institution, etc., and did a little bit of shopping. Had a bonser time. Came home by 4.40pm train, and then Ivy and I walked home from Goodna in the moonlight. Bought and read some new dialogues for proposed concert.

Sunday 18

Just got up before dinner, when Mr and Mrs Sandy Smith arrived, and they stayed until about 3.30pm, when Auntie Audrey, Ivy, and Zilpha and the Hilliers arrived and stayed until nearly 10. Dick McMahon called to see Dad. Brokenhearted!!!!!!!!

Monday 19

Got up real early and drove down to Goodna with Dad and back to school by train. Oh! hateful, hateful!! Got on alright in lessons, and had two preparations as chucked music now. Helped Jessie unpack, read, eat chocolate, and broke several rules this afternoon. To think of it being first day after Mid-winter holidays, Oh! horrible, horrible!! Studied until 9pm von da ab (tonight). Goodnight.

Tuesday 20

Terrible to have to get up so early these mornings. Simply beautiful not taking music, though! Had prep. all the afternoon. Was as sick as anything at dinnertime, but got alright afterwards. Most frightfully sleepy History lesson, but alright English. Read and talked to the Footes all the afternoon. The days are getting a bit longer now-a-days. Good job!

Wednesday 21

Got on well all day. Had a nice History lesson. Raining hard early this morning, and has been very gloomy all day. Played tennis for a while with Jessie and Muriel this afternoon, when I saw Mum and Mrs. James driving past, so Mum came in and had a bit of talk with her. Then I read the rest of the afternoon. Nothing else, rather late as we stay up until nine o'clock now.

Thursday 22

Had a very nice day considering everything. The time table is a bit altered. Got on fairly in German and Algebra. Then had prep. and then had a rather nice English lesson. Then had very nice Geography and History lessons. Then read in shed with Muriel and afterwards played tennis with her while a lot went for a walk. Jessie went down town to meet her auntie. Going home tomorrow, so goodbye.

Friday 23

Had a very nice day. Nothing special happened per usual. Got on alright in English and very well in German. Then had rather nice Gyms., but borrowed Hilda's suit and Jessie's shoes for the occasion. Drove home with Dad with the new sulky. Then Dad met Miss Shepherd and Audrey in Goodna and brought them home. Auntie Audrey, Zilpha and Thelma over at night to fix up about concert.

Saturday 24
Audrey and I had breakfast very late. Then fooled around a bit in morning. In afternoon, kids came over to practise their songs, and dialogue people came afterwards. Fixed up about the dialogue and Auntie Audrey and Zilpha and Leonie didn't go home until after nine o'clock. Merv went to Band of Hope picnic. Looked rather dull all day.

Sunday 25
Sandy Smith drove out in morning. I took Audrey over to Farm, and I came home before dinner, and Merv went over for Audrey at night. Raining all the afternoon. I did German.

Monday 26
Drove down with Dad, Merv, Audrey and Miss Shepherd to Goodna. Talking to Willie Mac., on station. Had a very nice day. Got on well in English and German and other lessons. Played tennis for a good while this afternoon with Jessie and Evelyn Horton. Feeling awfully down-hearted about lessons etc.. New girls' concert tonight.

Tuesday 27
Got on well in lessons. Not such a sick or sleepy History as generally on Tuesday. Also had a very nice English lesson. Had prep. all the afternoon, something bonser. Played tennis for a while with Evelyn, Muriel, and Jessie, then had to come up, as it has been raining nearly ever since. Books so nice. Wrote to Thelma this afternoon, and asked for a photo, as Hilda got one from her.

Wednesday 28
Had a very nice day. The week is going pretty slowly though. Got on well in all lessons. Got a good lot of lessons ahead. Played tennis for a little while this afternoon, with Muriel C., Phyllis C., and Ruth G.. Then read the rest of the time. Feeling rather anxious as Mum's letter asking for Jessie to come down hasn't arrived yet. Got a letter from Thelma and also a photo of herself. I simply love it. No more news. No rain today, although it rained very heavily last night. Dying for the end of the week to come.

Thursday 29

Got on pretty fair in German and also in Algebra. Then got a letter from Mum and Jessie also got her invitation, which she is accepting. Got on pretty well in prep. and had a very nice English lesson. Had a fair Geography lesson, and an awfully funny History. We got the "giggles". Heard that 4000 soldiers from Enoggera were having a route march to Ipswich today but didn't see anything of them. Dying for tomorrow to come.

Friday 30

Got on pretty all right. Had English Exam. in afternoon. Wouldn't like to say how I got on - just about indescribable. Then had rather nice gymnastics. Then, came down by train with Jessie C., and we talked to Mrs Pettinger, then got lollies and then talked to Jessie until Brisbane train came in with Dad, Miss Littley and Audrey. We all drove home, and Auntie Audrey and Ivy came over at night and talked concert and fixed dresses, lollies, etc. Miss Littley stayed at Farm all night.

Saturday 31

Got up fairly early. Then washed our heads and Jessie and I went down to Creek and got a glorious basket of wattle. At dinner time started to rain, and cleared up until about 5 o'clock when it stormed and stormed until about 8.30. It was astonishingly cruel. Allen B. and George A. arrived per bikes about 5 o'clock. Had to make best of bad job, as NO CONCERT.

Sunday 1

Ted Palmer arrived about 9 o'clock this morning. Then we all with Campbell's had picnic dinner at the Creek. Then came home and played tennis until before dark when boys went home. Linleys and Kerwicks were out, too. Mat. Kerwin over at night.

Monday 2

Got up very early. Dad took Miss Littley and Audrey back to Brisbane by 7.20 train. Mummy drove Jessie and me into school. Got here pretty late. Got on real well in English, then had alright other lessons. Played tennis on new courts with Jessie and Muriel this afternoon. Then read out on lawn for a good while, then went inside, and took transfer for Jessie and read. Miss Hill is rousing, so must get into bed. Goodnight.

Tuesday 3

Hardly prepared a lesson, but got on real alright all the same. Got on fairly in English, ditto in History. Had very nice Geography lesson this afternoon. Had meeting in Form Room to choose a Form Basket Ball Team. Then played tennis with Jessie and Muriel, and was beaten by J. (first time this year). Then I read war stories out of a magazine for rest of afternoon. Talking to Footes for a little while. Heard that Allen and George went down to Enoggera today.

Wednesday 4

Had prep. all the morning. Real bonser. Then had an alright History lesson and the most frightful Algebra Exam. I have ever seen (and got 8). I did not imagine that anything could be so awful. Got on alright in afternoon, but a big storm threatened, but it didn't come to very much. So off we trotted in the mud to the Town Hall to the meeting to attest our "inflexible determination to continue this way to a right and advantageous (victorious) end" or something of the sort. It was a lovely meeting with speeches, songs, etc.. Got home about 10.30pm.. Anniversary of Declaration of War of England upon Germany.

Thursday 5

Very sleepy early this morning, but soon got over it. Had a very nice German Grammar lesson, then went over Algebra Exam.. Had prep., then a most awful English lesson. Went over Exam., and Miss Lilley pegged away at me all the time, and then again when I didn't know my home lessons. Had first Geog. Exam., then alright History. Got a note and snaps from Ted. Palmer this afternoon. They are real nice. Read all afternoon, but a bit chilly. Got a home letter this afternoon.

179

Friday 6

Had an alright day. Had German Exam., and scored 29
some how or other, then had alright English. Had Arithmetic Exam. this afternoon, but don't know how I got on.
Then, fair gymnastics. Started to walk downtown after
school, but Mum caught me up and we shopped until after
dark. Saw "my darling" (otherwise Phyllis) in town, and
she gave me a beaming smile (I don't think). Miss Hebden
and Audrey came up, and Campbells and Hilliers also for a
rehearsal.

Saturday 7

Got up pretty late. Dad drove down to Goodna in
morning and brought home Miss Taylor. Audrey went
over to Farm for a little while. Didn't do much in the
afternoon. All drove over to Concert at night. Had a
nice time, but not nearly so nice as last time. Uncle
Willie (Campbell) also came over. Pa not at all well.
Merv went to a children's picnic at Woods' in afternoon.

Sunday 8

Didn't get up until dinnertime. May Hebden went
home in afternoon. Auntie Audrey, Evie and Thelma
Hillier and Edie Martin came over in afternoon.
Uncle Willie called up. Also a Mr. Simpson and Dick
McMahon.

Monday 9

Got up very early for Miss Taylor to catch 7.20 train,
but a big thunder storm was on, so waited until later
train. Audrey staying at home this week. Saw Bob.
Hebden at E. Ippy this morning, and spoke to him for a
minute or two. Got on alright in lessons. Had rather
nice English lesson and went over German Exam. (I
got 29). I played tennis for a while with Jessie and
won 21-14. Read and helped knit for rest of time.
Nothing else happened.

Tuesday 10

Most frightfully cold this morning. Got on alright in English, and a not too bad History hour lesson. Did Geography at dinner time and in prep., and then had Geography. No mail today, although expecting some. Playing tennis for a while with Jessie, and then talked to Foote's all the afternoon. Muriel Collin's birthday - 17 today. Allen and George went into Camp at Enoggera today. Wrote to Thelma a bit and also to Ted P. tonight. (but changed my mind, and didn't post them).

Wednesday 11

Most frightfully cold this morning and nearly all day. Had prep. all the morning. Then had a most frightful Exam. in History, and I never finished it either. (Got 36). Very nice algebra lesson. Then had an extra good arithmetic lesson. Miss Carm. evidently thinks I'm not the worst in the class after all. Played tennis for a while (compulsory) with Lillah Taylor, Queenie Morgan, and Marjorie Hall. Then read, and wrote or at least finished my letter to Thelma. Tried to finish off the kitten tonight, as have had enough of it. Going home tomorrow. Lovely!!

Thursday 12

Had an alright day concerning lessons, only I monopolised the whole of German lesson, as could not understand anything. Came home by 10 past 4 train, and while waiting for Mum, went down and bought some chocolates. Met Uncle Jim there. After Mum came, did a bit of shopping and Ivy drove home with us, (as she rode down). Picked Audrey up at Farm. I had a musical evening to myself, while Mum read out in kitchen to Audrey and Mr Chapman. Second lot of wounded soldiers arrived in Brisbane.

Friday 13

Got up awfully late and then had breakfast. Didn't want to go to Exhibition so stayed home. Just fooled around all day, and helped Mum address catalogues in afternoon. Mr Chapman came up for meals, as he is doing work up at new house. Mr Hazelmore promised to bring phonograph up tomorrow. That's all that happened. So I must shut up. Oh dear, oh, dear! Dreadful to have nothing to say.

Saturday 14

Got up very late again, and then had breakfast. Mum went over to Farm just after dinner, but we all did a good bit of work in morning. Ted Palmer turned up on bike this afternoon, and though he didn't intend to, he stayed all night. Mr Hazelmore brought his phonograph, and we tried nearly all the records tonight.

Sunday 15

Nothing doing in morning. But in afternoon, most of Farm people, as well as Mr and Mrs Malc. Campbell and Mr. and Mrs. and Lorna Hooper in motor, came. Played tennis in afternoon. Ted Palmer still here.

Monday 16

Got up much earlier than usual. Dad was in bed when we left with Influenza. He got bad last night. Mum took Audrey back to Bris. by 7.20 train. I saw Bob. Hebden, but couldn't say much. Got on well in English, and in other lessons. Played tennis for a while with Jessie this afternoon. Then I knitted for rest of time. My muffler getting on beautifully. I am very tired tonight. Result of getting up too early. Hilda gave me snap. of herself.

Tuesday 17

Got on really well, considering everything. Had nice Arithmetic and Algebra lessons, then nice English lesson, and then had an hour History lesson which wasn't sleepy at all. Had extra nice Geography lesson. Played tennis for a while with Jessie, and then knitted for rest of afternoon, but got it pulled out by Fatty and Jean, who were up to their pranks again today. Nearly sleeping in Hospital Dorm. on account of cat, but didn't.

Wednesday 18

Had prep. all morning, and got a good lot done. Then had nice History lesson, and then another terrible Algebra Exam., but scraped up 9 more marks than last time, managing to score the immense number of 17. Then had nice Arithmetic, and then prep.. Read, and talked to Jessie and Evelyn until 4.45, when I had to play basket ball. It was very nice, considering I didn't fall over or do anything undignified as usual. Came upstairs early with Eileen (without permission) and lay on her bed until 5.45. Tons of lessons for tomorrow. Just saw tail end of soldiers going to Front (in train) this morning.

Thursday 19

Thought I would peg out today with all my worries, but managed to get on alright. Had German first, and forgot all about it till the last minute, so of course, the result was an unearthly scramble. Then went over Algebra Exam., had prep., then nice English lesson. Then had Geography Exam., incidentally, didn't know a thing, and ditto in History, so had a very enjoyable time, thanks! Got a bonser letter from Thelma T. this morning. Played tennis, read and yarned this afternoon. Boys' Grammar Concert. (I didn't go)

Friday 20

Got on all right in morning, only on account of dog, had to have prep. in garden, and then had a most awful German Exam., and then very nice and tricky English Grammar lesson. Then most frightful Arithmetic Exam., and pretty nice Gymnastics. Came down in train with Miss Hodgens by myself (not Irish!). Uncle Willie drove me home. Mrs Prosser and Mrs Tucker up in car. Ted Palmer rode out.

Saturday 21

Mum slept with me last night, and neither of us got up very early. I rode over to Farm on bike in morning, saw Wedding cake finished, and came home after dinner. Didn't do much in afternoon. Dad was up all day today. At night, Mum, Auntie Audrey and I drove, Ivy rode, and Merv and Ted walked, to Bobby Bingo Social. Mostly dancing, as the games weren't much of a success.

Sunday 22
All got up very late. I learnt photography in morning and took some photos. Played tennis in afternoon. Linleys were out in car. Mrs Poor, Ivy also over. Ted Palmer went home. Mr Chapman came back tonight. Feeling most frightfully tired.

Monday 23
Got up pretty early and Dad, Mum and I all drove down to Goodna in cart. I caught usual train, and Mum was going on to Brisbane by next. Had nice English lesson then alright Arith. one. Then nice Geography. Had pretty nice German lesson. Went over Exam. by the way, I got 30 (scored 1 more than last time). A bit wet all afternoon, so no sports. I read a lovely book "Misunderstood", and a bit of a magazine. Got a headache tonight. Gave Miss White my parcel to post.

Tuesday 24
Pretty tired this morning. Got results of Arithmetic and Geography exams. 22 and 42 respectively. Had the most cruel English exam. I ever set eyes on. Pretty nice History lesson, and also nice Geography. Raining all day and especially pretty hard this afternoon. Miss White asked Jessie and me into her drawing room to study this afternoon, and we stayed there for over an hour.

Wednesday 25
A most glorious morning. Not a sprinkle of rain today. Had prep. all morning, then had a most frightful History exam.. I managed to get 31. Got photos and note from Ted Palmer this morning. I reckon I did well for first time (but don't think he did). Started "Indices" in Algebra today - the most absurd rot ever invented. Compulsory sports this afternoon, so played tennis on new courts with Edith England, Miriam Luck and Dorothy Creaser. Jessie had friend up to see her. Nearly killed with lessons for tomorrow. No home letter or parcel turned up so far.

Thursday 26

Another case of measles today. That's three now. Had fair German Grammar lesson, and alright Algebra. Rather nice English, pretty bad Geography and fair History. Got a home letter and parcel this morning. Read for a while and played tennis this afternoon, then talked to Jessie, Evelyn, Phyllis, Muriel and Eileen for rest of time. Not too well this morning. Feeling dumpy about not packing up to go home tomorrow. Goodnight.

Friday 27

Got on alright all day. Prep. all morning, then rather nice German, and pretty fair English lessons. Had very early time table. Had another Arith. Exam., but don't think I did any better (if not worse) than last time. Watched tennis match against High School (Bris.) this afternoon, and was excused from gymnastics. Then knitted rest of time. Horrible not going home, but not nearly as bad as I thought it would be. Am in a fix about tomorrow.

Saturday 28 Queensland Day

Went down early with Jessie and Miss Carmody to see procession. Then went to N. Ipswich Sports Grounds. Ivy's birthday. Had a bonser day. Raffled Red Cross Doll. Came home about 10 o'clock at night. Hired a car and motored home in moonlight. It was lovely. Ted P. came out with us. Very sick in afternoon, but alright afterwards.

Sunday 29

Didn't get up until nearly dinnertime. No visitors in afternoon, but Ivy, Ma and Tom called up for a few minutes. Very very tired and have neuralgia. Have done hardly any lessons or anything.

Monday 30

Got up much later than usual, and left home later than I ever did before. Mum drove me into town. Had fair English, and an awfully amusing Arith. lesson, as Miss Carmody tried to stand on her dignity. Had very nice Geography and rather stale German lessons. Miss White made me change coloured collar at dinner time. Found I am "defender" in Form Basket Ball Team. Rotten!! Played tennis this afternoon, and talked the rest of the time. Wrote to Audrey and did some knitting.

Tuesday 31

Had very nice Arith. and Algebra lessons. Then fair English, and not a bit sleepy History lesson, as I giggled all the time. Very nice Geography, only that the kids have gone mad teasing me today (without reason) and making me frightfully embarrassed. Played tennis this afternoon, and knitted rest of time. Didn't do any study tonight, as we talked about Mormons all the time.

Wednesday 1

Had alright day, only that I was as sick as anything about dinnertime, but cheered up this afternoon. Awfully sleepy history lesson, but a bit better Algebra Exam., for which I got 22 (highest so far this term). A pretty awful Arith. lesson. Finished all my wool this afternoon for my knitting, and then had to play Basket Ball (Compulsory). Got a short letter from home this afternoon. Very late, so had better shut off. Goodnight.

Thursday 2

Had an alright day, per usual. Had a very tricky German lesson, when Miss White took a bad or mad turn, then went over Algebra Exam.. Had fair English lesson, when we went over Exam.. then had Geography Exam., but I didn't like it. Rather fair History lesson. Had to umpire for basket ball for a good while this afternoon. Then I read out war stories for rest of time. Glad I'm going home tomorrow. Saw in Q.T. where some rel. of Williamson's died at Plains yesterday.

Friday 3

Had pretty fair day. Had rather awful German Exam., though. I only got 26. Good job, last Exam.. Alright other lessons. Mum called for me some time after four and gave me snaps of "soldier boys". Called at Linley's going home. Dad went down to Bris. for Audrey. We got home first and got tea ready. Went to bed soon after, but that was pretty late. A frightfully hot day and also hot night.

Saturday 4

Got up in decent time. Ivy came over in morning, and told us Social was put off as old Mr. Kerwin from the Creek died last night. We worked all day. In afternoon, Audrey and I made a chocolate pudding, Queen's biscuits, and sugar candy, and all were a great success. Mr. Chappel arrived at night, and stayed all night.

Sunday 5

Sandy Smith's out in morning, also Messrs. Harbottle and Denty. Mum went to Mr. Kerwin's funeral, so I had to preside at dinner. Mr. Chappel went away. Audrey and I drove as far as Farm with Smith's this afternoon for a while.

Monday 6

Not quite so bad getting up early this morning, as not as cold as usual. Drove to Goodna with Dad, Merv. and Audrey. Posted my letter on G. station. Dad took Audrey to Bris.. Speaking to Eva Warner for a while on station. Saw B. T. also. Had alright lessons. Played tennis this afternoon for a while, and then did some lessons. Nearly killed with work for tomorrow and have a horrible headache and neuralgia now.

Tuesday 7

Had nice arithmetic and Algebra lessons. Then had what would have been a nice Exam., if it hadn't been so jolly long. I didn't fall in love with it. Then had alright History. They are not so sleepy lately. Had an extra nice Geography lesson. Raining in fits and starts this afternoon. I played tennis this afternoon for a while, then fool in Form room with Eileen, etc., then had a talk in garden, then wrote a long letter to Thelma.

Wednesday 8

Got up a bit earlier than usual, and stewed History. Did History in Preps. in morning, then had Exam.. I couldn't stand it, didn't even get finished. Had alright Algebra lesson. Had neuralgia something frightfully this morning, and also came on tonight again a bit. Had very nice afternoon. Wonder of wonders, didn't have to play basket ball, but nearly had to. Only Phyllis Cos. and I scraped out of it. Got 35 for History - not too bad. Got a letter from Ted Palmer this afternoon. Started to read "Little Men". I think it is lovely. Goodnight.

Thursday 9

Had a fair day. Had pretty good German lesson and alright Algebra. Fair English, nice Geography, and pretty sleepy History lessons. Awfully close and suffocating heat today. Played tennis with Jessie this afternoon, then did some of Phyllis' knitting and talked to Evelyn. Didn't get a home letter. Read a good lot of "Little Men". Saw Dad go past this afternoon, but he didn't spot me. Goodnight.

Friday 10

Had pretty alright nice day for lessons. Had a horrible German lesson though. Had Arithmetic Exam. this afternoon - last exam. this term. Got two letters this morning - one from Auntie Audrey and one from Thelma. Didn't go down until 5.20 train. Had a talk to Cissy Pettinger on Goodna platform. Then waited for Audrey and Miss Taylor in next train with Merv. Campbell's went up to new house today.

Saturday 11

Got up fairly early. Then before dinner, Audrey and I went up to Pentwyn. First visit there, and I thought it was very nice. Didn't do much else. Five big hail thunderstorms in succession, which started about 4 and lasted till 7. 105 points. Had gramophone nearly all afternoon, and read out to Audrey at night.

Sunday 12

I wrote to Myfanwy, asking her down. A Mr McGee and son were here for dinner, etc.. Jim Rice and Billy Johnstone over in afternoon. Audrey and I went to Pentwyn in morning and Mum and Miss Taylor in afternoon.

Monday 13

Drove down to Goodna with Dad in sulky. Talking to Con. Nahrung for a while. Saw, and got a glorious smile from, Mr Jones, our old Book-keeping teacher in Dinmore Station. Got on well in English and Geography and likewise in German. Never took any exercise this afternoon. Started, and have almost finished "The Little Green Door". I think it is beautiful. Nothing else, goodnight.

Tuesday 14

Finished the "Little Green Door". Had rather nice exciting English lesson, as Dorothy played up a bit. Had a sleepy History lesson, and haven't got over it yet. Went down to E. Ipswich station for a parcel, with Jessie, and had some bonser chocolate and cake. Miss White took us for study tonight as she copped us talking, etc.. Practised some basket ball this morning for match tomorrow (beg your parding!)

Wednesday 15

Had a very easy going day, and got tons of lessons ahead. Read Shakespeare with Dorothy McGill and Edna Hadley at dinner time. Then donned a Basket Ball rigout this afternoon, and we played our first match. We played well, but were defeated - 43 to 9, by Lower V. I was defender, and oh! I never wish to see the game again as long as I live. I fell over twice and as the consequence, I have my knee bandaged up, and my stockings in holes. Nothing else doing. Goodnight. Had to study in School Hall - Rotten!!!

Thursday 16

Got on very well all day, only have a sore stiff knee, stiff body and dislocated finger. Had a very nice German lesson, and pretty fair English. Had also very nice Geography and a sleepy don't -care History lesson. Never did a thing but lie about and talk this afternoon. Jessie had a very stiff neck. A storm threatened tonight, but didn't turn up. Goodnight. Most frightfully hot.

Friday 17

Had a pretty nice day. Got on fairly in all lessons. Met Mum at gates, and (unexpectedly) she took me into town, and we didn't leave until six, and got home at eight. I never looked so disreputable in my life. Dad and Merv. had started out to look for us, but we're bad eggs alright and turned up. Went to bed about half past nine. Nothing else happened.

Saturday 18

Got up reasonably early. Worked fairly hard in morning. Mrs Armstrong, Miss Crookston, and Mr Woods came out in morning. I read and played piano in afternoon. Ivy (little) (daughter of Will and Laura Campbell) went into Hospital with pneumonia. Daddy went to meeting in Bris. tonight. I painted and read until very late.

Sunday 19

Got up early. Had easy day. Mr. and Mrs. Tom Smith drove out in afternoon. Mat. Kerwin over at night and took Dick's Cake - I got my silver-mounted jelly dish - awfully nice.

Monday 20

Got up early as usual on Monday morning. Drove down to Goodna with Dad with Larry in sulky. Got up to school alright, but am frightfully sick of it. Had alright lessons. Jessie up today for first time. I talked and did a little Geography with Edna Hadley this afternoon. I started "Pollyanna Grows Up" tonight. Got tons of lessons for to-morrow. Been eating cream puffs, chocolates and different kinds of iced cake today as well as toffee.

Tuesday 21

Had a very uninteresting day. Dragged through all les-sons somehow. Lot of kids sick in Hospital Dorm.. Frightfully sleepy History lesson, alright others. Teacher's Meeting this afternoon. I read out and talked to Jessie, Eileen and the two Foote's. Didn't do a thing in study tonight, hardly. Am most frightfully sleepy.

Wednesday 22

Big storm last night, and rained a lot today. Did a good deal of Expansion revision. Had alright lessons. As it was raining, no sports this afternoon and therefore I didn't play in the hateful Basket Ball Match. Read ever so much of "Pollyanna Grows Up" instead. Most frightfully sleepy and everything, and in a hurry to read some more, so must shut up. How many times have I blessed this paragraph! Well, here's another blessing for it. I'll take care to have more to talk about next year, so I will!!!!

Thursday 23

Had very nice lessons today. I finished reading "Pollyanna Grows Up". I think it's just lovely. Read a story out of a magazine. Watched Basket Ball Match most of afternoon. Then had a look at Miss Wood's wedding presents and then wrote part of letter to Thelma. Put some "Good Luck" Coupons on Miss Wood's table for last night here.

Friday 24

Had very nice lessons most of day. Then came down by 4.15 train and waited on station in Goodna until about half past 5, when Mum came for me. I was talking to Eva Warner and she introduced me to Miss Gibson who asked me up for a week-end. Mum drove me home and I went to bed fairly early. Goodnight.

Saturday 25

Got up pretty early. Before dinner, two motor loads of teachers came out to see the Apiary. Audrey came up with Institution teachers this morning. They all went home after 4 o'clock. At night, Dad, Auntie Audrey, Ivy and I went to Farewell Social to Goodna volunteers in Asylum Hall. Heard of Dr O'Brien's death yesterday.

Sunday 26

Didn't get up until about dinnertime. In afternoon Mr and Tom Waghorn and Ted Palmer were here, also Campbell girls came up, and we had a bit of music etc., at night.

Monday 27

Lovely not having to go back to school. Mum washed nearly all day. Auntie Audrey came up before dinner, and stayed until late in afternoon, when Mum and I went home with her to fit my dress on, etc.. I studied all day, but only got about 30 pages of Expansion done all the same. Nothing much doing, so can't fill up more space. Audrey and Miss Shepherd went back to Institution this morning, so all on my lonely. Got a letter from Eileen.

Tuesday 28

I studied in the morning again today, but didn't get as much done today as yesterday. At night, Mr and Tom Waghorn came up, and Mum, Merv and I went home with them. Auntie Audrey did some more to my dress, and we spent a good part of the evening there. Ivy started a new term of Dressmaking again today. Got a letter from Jessie.

Wednesday 29

Didn't do much in morning, but before dinner I did some studying, and then when mail and Barnsies' photos came I took them up to the New place. I stayed until nearly tea-time. Mum came up in afternoon, and we went home together. Auntie Laura went to Ipswich and brought little Ivy home from Hospital. Mr Waghorn left this morning. Ivy went up to Dressmaking again today, and had a test Exam.. Nothing else, so goodnight and good luck.

Thursday 30

Went down to Goodna in cart with Dad and then up to Ipswich by myself in train this morning. Mum drove in and met me in town. Shopped nearly all day. Met George and Allen in uniform and had a talk to them in afternoon. Then I went up to Barnet's and had a tooth out. Then we drove home, and no bad after effects of my tooth. Got home about dark and Ivy and Auntie Audrey came up at night for a while.

Friday 1

Dad and Auntie Audrey away in Bris. nearly all day. Got up fairly early. Nothing doing all day. In afternoon tried to arrange something for soldier boys tomorrow night, and had great fun with it. Went up to Campbell's for tea and most of evening, and then Ivy and Auntie Audrey came back and spent rest of evening with us and arranged speeches etc.. Merv went to Holland's for soft drinks.

Saturday 2

Got up decently early. Fooled round and did a good bit of work in morning. Then after dinner Ivy and A. Audrey came up. About 3.30, Allen and Ted arrived - minus George, who had a bad cold. Played tennis in afternoon, had a bonser tea and then had dancing, music, recitations, speeches and gases, for rest of evening. Got a "Rising Sun". Awfully pleased.

Sunday 3

Allen and Ted went about 8.30am. Also Miss Taylor went early away. We went up to Campbells in afternoon, where we met Mrs. and Jessie Brennan. Talked over yesterday, etc..

Monday 4

Got up early as Audrey went back to school with Dad. I then went up to Campbell's and brought Ivy back with me, and she stayed all day, and helped Mummy make me a new school dress. Barnsies came up in afternoon, and Ivors went home with Ivy. I studied nearly all day. Just simply hate the thought of going back tomorrow. Went to bed early, as no more sleep for a week. Eight Hour Day in Ipswich.

Tuesday 5

Got up early and drove down to Goodna in sulky with Dad and Merv, and then came on to school by train. Had a very nice day. Got on real well in all lessons. Talking to Footes nearly all afternoon, and got the life teased out of me about T.P.. Then we ran about a bit to take exercise. Pretty cold this afternoon, so hope I won't be shivering in bed.

Wednesday 6

Got up extra early, and started studying. Had a biscuit in study this morning, as Miss White shouted us a tinful to eat. Did a lot of History revision and got on well in all lessons. Didn't take any exercise this afternoon. Gymnastic competition too this afternoon, but I didn't watch it. Jessie has a funny rash all over her, so is sleeping in Hospital Dorm.. I wrote to Thelma Tritton today. Not feeling a bit happy. Am feeling homesick and a bit funny altogether. Goodnight. Most of us sent up to bed early for talking in study.

Thursday 7

Had a nice day. Got on well in German and Algebra, and every other lesson. The day passed quickly for a wonder. Edna Hadley went home, so I had to play in her place in a Form Tennis Match. We won by about 48 points. Jessie was worse this morning, but is feeling better tonight. I can't get my work ahead, no matter how I try. Didn't get a home letter today. Goodnight.

Friday 8

Had a very fair day altogether. Had nice lessons, and thank goodness! no more gymnastics. Mum and Mrs Parry called for me long before I was ready to drive home. Ted P. rang up to hurry. Merv drove to Goodna for Miss Shepherd and Audrey. I went up to Campbell's and Auntie Audrey and Ivy, Zilpha Hillier and (Private Stanford) Josey came home with me and spent the evening.

Saturday 9

Got up fair to middling early. Then after tidying up, Audrey and I went up to Campbells and stayed all day to get our dresses fixed up and finished. Miss Shepherd also came up for the afternoon. Nothing doing at night, so all went to bed early. I did some study this afternoon.

Sunday 10

Mr Bunnet and Ted P. came out this morning and went home after dinner. In afternoon, Private Jimmy Josey, and Miss Hillier, Mr and Miss Albury, Auntie Audrey, Ivy, Kon Nahrung and Jim Gibson were out.

Monday 11

Drove down early with Dad, Miss Shepherd and Audrey, to catch the 7.20 train. I came up to school by train and had the agony of our first Tests. Had Arithmetic this morning, and English this afternoon. Liked English far better than Arith. (and I'd need to). I am blissfully in ignorance of Algebra and History for tomorrow. Can't help it.

194

Tuesday 12

Got up very early. Had a most frightful Algebra Exam. this morning, and a cruel History one this afternoon. Thank Goodness, they're over! Did a good lot of my "Folly" dress for Saturday, today. Talked to Girlie Foote for a while this afternoon, and heard some startling things! Then four of us went for a walk to town, where Helen (Miss White) caught us and brought us home.

Wednesday 13

Never had any lessons this morning, as other kids had Geometry tests. So Edna, Dorothy, Marjorie, Ida and I did first History and then Geography out in the shed. History and Algebra came out. I got 64 and 33. Had Geography Tests this afternoon while other kids had Greek. The paper was only fair. I sewed all the afternoon at my "Folly" dress, but didn't get extra much done, and am in a bit of a mess. Posted a letter to Mum this morning. No Exams. tomorrow, thank goodness! Goodnight!!!

Thursday 14

Only had three quarters of an hour lesson this afternoon, as had Prep. this morning, as others had Latin Exam. and then Geography lesson. Talked to Marj. Foote nearly all afternoon. Went down to E. Ipswich with Jessie for a parcel. Mum drove up to see me, and brought me some things. Got most of my dress done today by dress-maker.

Friday 15

Had German Exam.. It was pretty bad!! Then we had Arithmetic and Latin lessons this afternoon. Saw Marj. Foote for a few minutes. Helped Miss Lilley decorate ice-cream stall, went over to tuck shop for string, etc.. Finished my "Folly" dress altogether. Does seem funny not going home tonight.

Saturday 16

Prepared for Bazaar in morning, cutting up fruit for salad, making ice creams, decorating stalls, etc.. Had bazaar in afternoon. Deadliest thing I was ever at. Then had Ball at night. Had a scrumptious time. Had an awfully pleasant surprise as Allen B. was there. He looked bons. in his uniform, and was awfully nice.

Sunday 17

Went home by 7.30 am train from E. Ippie. Merv drove me home from Goodna. Was sick all day, and slept nearly all the time. Mr. and Mrs. Sandy Smith and Kon. Nahrung were out. Ivy and A. Audrey came up.

Monday 18

Came back to school per usual by train - pretty sick in morning, but alright now. Got on well in all lessons. Went over English tests, and Miss Lilley quite calm about them. Did a bit of German and talked to Eileen and Jessie this afternoon. Hardly did a thing in study, as was so tired. I slept most of time. I'm fearfully sleepy. Goodnight.

Tuesday 19

Had a pretty alright day. Nothing exciting happened. Had not a very nice English lesson, but a very horrid History hour lesson. Foote's didn't turn up this afternoon, so nothing startling in that direction. Got a letter from Mum this afternoon, asking me how I was. Am still sleepy, although I pretty well slept nearly all the afternoon.

Wednesday 20

Nothing wonderful happened. Posted a letter home to Mum this morning. Had a little touch of my old complaint today, but took care Mum's instructions. Had an awfully sleepy history lesson, and an awfully exciting Arithmetic one, as Dorothy McGill and Miss Carm. had a "bust-up", and we were kept in after school to finish the lesson. Had to umpire for a form tennis match this afternoon, and then lay on grass and talked and slept rest of time. Miss White fussing round at bed time. Goodnight and good luck.

Thursday 21

Had not extra nice day. Pretty fair German and Algebra lessons. Then not very nice English one. Alright Geography but the rottenest History lesson I ever remember having. Mum came up to see me this afternoon. George and Allen left for Front today by boat. A most glorious moonlight night (good omen for our boys).

Friday 22

Had a very nice day. Got on alright in lessons. Went home by quarter past four train, and waited on Goodna station until 20 past 5, when Mum and Audrey came home from Brisbane. We all drove home together. Ivy and Auntie Audrey came up at night for a while. After they went, had a bit of music, and then went to bed.

Saturday 23

Got up fairly early for a wonder. Audrey and I never did anything much all day. Dad went to Beekeepers' Meeting in Bris. at night. In evening, Ted Palmer arrived per bike. We and Campbells went over to musical evening at James' at night. Had a nice time.

Sunday 24

Menfolk went to O'possum Creek in morning, Audrey went up to Campbells, and I rode up on bike. Campbells down in afternoon and played tennis and had some music at night. James and friends over in afternoon.

Monday 25

Got up very early and Merv drove Mum, Audrey and me down to Goodna and I came on to school by train, and mum took Audrey back. Ted Palmer went home early this morning. I had a very fair day. Miss Lilley had the biggest "little outbreak" she has had for ever so long. Slept or pretty near it all the afternoon, but had a little tennis because we had to. Nothing else.

Tuesday 26

Got up very early. Had the sleepiest English lesson I ever remember having. It was agony. History was nearly as bad. Had nice afternoon lessons. Slept by myself until about quarter to five. Then came up and talked to Footes until tea bell went. Heard several startling facts. Was a bit sick and headachy today. Still most frightfully sleepy.

Wednesday 27
Very sleepy this morning, but that's me (?) now-a-days. Had a very nice lesson day. Had a very good History lesson, and also nice Algebra and Arith. lessons. Had last prep. in shed with Edna Hadley, and then studied with her all the rest of the afternoon. Most horribly windy today, and hot and close too. Got new tin of biscuits this morning. Nothing else much happened. I never get a letter or anything nowadays, I suppose because I don't write any. Goodnight.

Thursday 28
Had a pretty queer German lesson, and didn't enjoy Algebra much. Had pretty fair English lesson. Studied in Studio with Edna at dinnertime. Had nice Geography, but pretty horrid History lesson. Studied this afternoon with Edna, and then talked etc., from about five o'clock. Got a post card from Mum this morning, saying to meet her in town.

Friday 29
Had a very fair day, but horror of horrors, the Inspector came. He didn't take any of my subjects, for a good thing. I went down town with Edna Hadley this afternoon and met Mum and Merv. I had my "physogue" taken; and we did a good lot of shopping. Didn't come home until all hours. Called at Palmer's on the way home. Went to bed pretty early.

Saturday 30
Didn't get up very early. Ivy and Auntie Audrey came up early for a while in morning. It was the hottest and smokiest and pestiest day I've ever known. Bush-fires all around, to say nothing of flies. Mum made me a new blouse. I wrote a story. Ivy and Auntie Audrey came up at night and spent the evening.

Sunday 31
Mr (Sandy) Smith came out early in morning, and he and Dad and Merv went out to Creek. Kon. Nahrung came out to play tennis in afternoon. Ivy, Auntie Audrey and Zilpha Hillier over also.

Monday 1

Drove down to Goodna with Dad and Merv, and came up by train. Speaking to Morgan in train at station. Had a pretty fair day. Inspector (Mr Roe) still here, but thank goodness! hasn't taken me for anything yet. Did some History with Edna Hadley this afternoon and then talked, etc. for rest of time. Nothing else happened. Goodnight.

Tuesday 2

Had a very fair day, only horribly sleepy English and History lessons. Had nice other lessons. Inspector didn't turn up today, but daresay he will tomorrow. Saw Merv go past on bike this afternoon, but the mingy thing wouldn't look. Studied History with Edna again this afternoon. Getting awfully good lately!!!

Wednesday 3

Had extra Arith. lesson this morning with Eileen. Had nice morning, I got a letter from Thelma T. this morning. Had fairly nice History lesson, and nice Algebra. Had a very nice Arithmetic lesson, and went into Garden for next Prep. with Edna. Read History all afternoon with Edna H.. Nothing at all wonderful happened. Got Jessie to ring up and see if Morgan were in St. Andrew's yet, but he isn't so I found out. Hope to goodness tomorrow goes quickly. Goodnight.

Thursday 4

Had fair German and Algebra lessons. Then had alright English one. Had nice Geography but pretty awful History lesson, started very badly but ended up nicely. It was a most horribly hot, smoky and dusty day. Studied with Edna this afternoon for a while, and then talked rest of time. "Didn't get no letters nor nothing". Goodnight.

Friday 5

Had a fairly nice day. Nothing much happened. Had alright German, English and Arithmetic lessons etc.. Went home by usual train this afternoon. Waited for Dad and Audrey in next train, and then we drove home together. Talking to Muriel and Jack Jones on Station. Morgan getting on well. Nothing else.

Saturday 6
Mum went over to Hilliers with Auntie Audrey this morning
to decorate etc., while Audrey and I stayed at home and
slaved. Ivy came up in afternoon. We all went over to
Farewell Social to a lot of soldier boys (including Meyrick)
at Hilliers. Had a fair to middling time.

Sunday 7
Audrey and I didn't wake till nearly half past eleven. Sam
Rice came over in morning. Ivy and Auntie Audrey were up
for dinner.

Monday 8
Got up very early and drove down to Goodna with Dad,
Merv, and Audrey. Saw them off (except Merv) and then
came up by train per usual. Had a fair day. Had middling good English, nice German and other lessons.
Ethel and Ida had row with Carm. in Arith.. Nothing else
doing. Did some History with Edna and Jessie this afternoon, and then talked. I wish I could write about
something. Goodnight.

Tuesday 9
Had a pretty fair day. Alright Arith. and Algebra lessons.
Not extra nice English, as Marcie and Ethel got into hot
water about the blinds. Pretty awful History lesson, too. Bit
of a storm this afternoon. It came down heavily for two or
three minutes, but that was about all. Studied all afternoon in Form room.

Wednesday 10
Had prep first two lessons per usual. Then had a most fear-
some History lesson, as "Helen" stuck at me to answer a
question that I didn't know for fully half the lesson. Then
had rather a nice Algebra lesson. Rather nice Arith.
lesson. Then did a lot of History in shed with Edna. Went to
a Debating meeting in shed this afternoon. Subject,
"Should Conscription be put into force during the War".
Against it, won. I voted differently. Then did some more
lessons in garden afterwards.

Thursday 11

Had a most horrible German lesson. One kid couldn't answer so had to waste all lesson and make it up next Thursday instead. Had alright other lessons, including pretty fair English and a nice History (for a wonder). Miss White read out the marks for the term. Did a little tiny few lessons this afternoon. Then talked rest of time.

Friday 12

Had an alright, usual day. Had per usual lessons, not extra bad and of course not extra good.   Pretty long storm at school this afternoon. Got a home letter this afternoon. Dad and Merv called for me at about nine p.m., and then we drove home together and landed here about 11.20 pm. Had some soft drink, buns, etc. on way out.

Saturday 13

Got up pretty fairly early. Fooled around all morning. Ivy came up and stayed all day to study for her exam.. It was frightfully hot. Hilliers and Edie Martin and Auntie Audrey came over in afternoon for rehearsal for concert. Edie Martin stayed all night. Had a bit of music at night.

Sunday 14

Sam Rice and Lou. Llewellyn were over in morning. Zilpha Hillier, Dave Murray, Auntie Audrey, Mr and Miss Kerwick and a little boy out. Did hardly anything. Had a game of tennis.

Monday 15

Drove down to Goodna with Daddy and Merv. Then came up to school by train. Last Monday school I'll ever have! Hurrah for Casey!! Got on well in English and did a good many lessons. Had nice and uncommon German lesson. Miss White superintended our study tonight and sent us all to bed early, as an imposition for talking in study. Miss Hill just in to stop our noise, so better shut up.

201

Tuesday 16

Had a very nice day. Had nice English and then an extra nice History lesson, whatever happened. Girlie and Marj. Foote up this afternoon, and took some snaps of me. Then I wrote two letters - one to Morgan and one to Thelma Tritton. Eileen got news tonight that her uncle was burned to death. Today is the last whole day's school I am ever to have. Goodnight.

Wednesday 17

Last school I'm ever to have, I suppose. Only had half day school. Had one of the rottenest History lessons we've ever had, but a nice Algebra to finish up with. Never had any lessons this afternoon, but I studied a good bit of Algebra and then copied out a lovely account of the landing at Gallipoli. Looked out for Dad and Merv this afternoon, but they didn't turn up until tea time, when I just had a very little converse. with Merv. Miss White in an awful humour today, and is in bed pretty sick tonight.

Thursday 18

Did English all day, "Quentin Durward" in morning, and "Richard III" in afternoon. Mary and Girlie Foote were up in afternoon, and brought up the snaps they took on Tuesday. They are breaks ups altogether. Some of us joined together and got some fancy biscuits and chocolates at tuck-shop by day girl. Feeling awfully queer tonight - giddy and everything swimming around, although everything else alright. Had extra German lesson this morning.

Friday 19

Don't get up so early nowadays, although I ought to. Studied History all day and now I haven't finished it. It's just simply appalling to think of the Junior being so close, but it's worse to think of not going home tonight. It's something horrible. We had to defend our room against Lower V today and tonight. Had great sport, only other kids got an imposition from Carm..

Saturday 20

Studied, or at least tried to, all the morning. Jessie got a parcel, so shared contents of that. Went with V and VI Form girls to Miss Cribb's picnic in afternoon. Had a glorious time. Had a bonser walk while there. Then coming home we had an accident, and were stranded for about half an hour. Came home in moonlight.

Sunday 21

Went home early by train, and Merv met me at station and drove me home. Hadn't one visitor. Went up to Farm at night with Mum, Audrey and Miss Taylor.

Monday 22

Audrey and Miss Taylor went back to school early in morning. I did lessons in morning, had a sleep about dinner time, and then did a few more lessons. Merv drove me down to 20 past 5 train this afternoon, and I came up to school with Eileen. Got a letter from Thelma wishing me luck in the Junior. Studied tonight and had cream puffs for supper (miracle of miracles). Feeling shaky about my great stock of knowledge for tomorrow.

Tuesday 23

A memorable day today alright. Our Junior started. Had "Compulsory" in morning, which I perhaps passed in and English in the afternoon, which I certainly failed in. It was a most abominable paper. Didn't get a bit nervous or flurried, thank goodness!! Miss Carmody took all of us "Juniors" over to tuck shop tonight, where we all had an ice drink and some lollies.

Wednesday 24

Did a few lessons in morning, although not supposed to. Just as well I did, as I got some of the things I looked up in Geography. Had Arithmetic in morning, and think I only got one sum right. Failed sure as eggs. Had Geography in afternoon. I liked that better, and I should have passed in that. Saw the Footes for a few minutes in morning. Bought some Chiclets to eat. Looking forward to a hateful day tomorrow. Goodnight.

Thursday 25

Had a nice Algebra lesson in morning, but of course I couldn't do anything. Then came home for dinner, and in afternoon had a pretty fair History Exam. I was coming home (after being refreshed at Whitehouse's) and met Mum, so, as she had my basket, we went into town. Had tea with Ted P.. Came home to meeting in school, where met Dad, who drove us home.

Friday 26

Did hardly a thing all morning, as Ivy, Aunties Laura and Audrey came up, and we all talked. Then painted, read, etc. in afternoon, and only did a few lessons early in morning. Had a very easy day altogether. Had some music to myself in evening. Nothing else doing, so goodnight.

Saturday 27

Didn't do very much lessons in morning, but did more in afternoon. Went to sleep, though, in afternoon while doing my lessons. Read a little tonight. Mum took all curtains down, washed and everything in an uproar. So, goodnight. Sam Rice and family over in evening.

Sunday 28

Didn't do much lessons today, although tried to. Read a bonser story in a magazine, "The Lone Wolf". Went to bed early. Evie and Esther Hillier over in afternoon.

Monday 29

Got up fairly early. Dad, Merv, and some Farm people went to Goodna, where they are entertaining the "Dungaree Recruits" at dinner on river bank. I didn't really get up, until just before I left. Ma came up, and had dinner with us. Merv drove me down to Goodna like mad, but got me there on time for train. Came up with Eileen in 5.20pm train.

Tuesday 30

Had a horrid German Exam. this morning, but thank goodness! it's the last of my Junior subjects. Read all the afternoon in the garden, then talked to Footes and Edna Hadley. Disposed of my coconut ice, and some of my cake. Read a lot of "Guy Mannering".

Wednesday 1

Had a very lovely lazy day. Never did a thing (hardly) but read all day. Jessie and I went down town this afternoon to do some shopping. We saw Morgan there. Got some fancy work this afternoon at Cribb's and have done quite a lot already. Nothing else wonderful happened. Can't imagine I've left school. I do wish I might make up something to fill up space.

Thursday 2

Got up a bit early to sew. Then kept on sewing all day, and quite finished my d'oyley. I am quite proud of it. This afternoon Miss White took all Junior and Senior examinees of both Boys' and Girls' School, to a spread in Whitehouses. We had a bonser time. Read all tonight in Boarders' Sitting-Room, but most of kids went out. Looking forward to going home.

Friday 3

Passed another nice quiet, peaceable day in the shed, reading. Read quite a lot of "Guy Mannering". Went home by usual train with Jessie. Morgan took us for a drive round the Asylum. Mum brought Audrey home from Bris.. Didn't do much at night. Read, talked and fooled around generally before going to bed.

Saturday 4

We all cooked nearly all the morning. Jessie and I made biscuits and cakes, and Audrey made tarts. Merv went to Goodna and met Myfanwy Parry. Later, Elwin Parry and Ted Palmer arrived. We had a set of tennis just before dark, and had music, dancing and fooling at night. Zilpha and Campbells over.

Sunday 5

Played some tennis in morning then Ted, Elwyn, Jessie, Vonnie and I went up to Campbells. Had more tennis in afternoon, and music at night. Ted and Elwyn went home early. Zilpha, Campbells, Kon. Nahrung and Jim Gibson were out. (Terribly shocked and disappointed.)

Monday 6

Mum took Audrey back to school early. Vonnie also went
back at same time. Jessie and I fooled round, after getting
up late. Mum got home about 12 o'clock. Washed my head,
bathed etc in afternoon. Ma came up for a while. Mum
wrote to engage a room at Manly for Xmas. I have a
bonser cold.

Tuesday 7

Came back by usual early train from Goodna, with Jessie.
Saw Morgan and Cissie Pettinger on platform. Read nearly
all day. Have pretty nearly finished "Guy Mannering".
Had fancy dress tea at night. I went as "housemaid". Then
afterwards V Form gave a concert. It was enjoyed by all
very much.

Wednesday 8

Got up early and finished "Guy Mannering" this morning.
Then rest of time until dinner helped to make fruit salad.
This afternoon helped fix stalls etc,. until 4 o'clock, when the
Bazaar Affair, in aid of Comforts for Wounded Soldiers was
opened. I was a "Folly" in ice-cream stall. Tonight there
was a concert in front of school. It was fairly good, but very
stale at times. Can't imagine this is my last whole day at
school.

Thursday 9

Fooled round in morning, then got awfully sick - deadly, in
fact. Mum and Merv called up to see me in morning. Missed
my dinner, as was so sick. Miss White made me go to
"Breaking-Up" at Boys' Grammar, although I didn't want
to. We all went up in cabs. Met Mum and Merv there. Then,
after afternoon tea, we drove home together. I got pretty
right once I started. Last day's school.

Friday 10

Mum went down in morning to Brisbane to bring Audrey
home. I took mail up to "Farm", stayed for dinner, etc.,
until about 3 o'clock, when Ivy came home with me. Mum
and Audrey arrived about six o'clock. Aunties Audrey and
Ivy came up at night to fix about house for tomorrow.

Saturday 11

Great day of prayer for peace, and the sins of the nation. Ivy went down to Cathedral. I fooled round. Auntie Audrey and Audrey went to Goodna and met Private J Cooms. Then he and Aunties Audrey and Laura came up at night, and we had a nice evening.

Sunday 12

Audrey went up to Farm for dinner. Ivy and I came back early then others came, had tea here, and drove Pte Cooms back to train afterwards.

Monday 13

Got up very late. Tried on new bathing suits, then had dinner. Read out nearly all the afternoon "Kenilworth" to Audrey. Mum sewed all day. Auntie Audrey took the two little Barnsie girls (Ivors and Audrey) to Brisbane. Dad went to a Committee meeting in school at night. First real day's holiday.

Tuesday 14

Got up pretty late. The two "Bills" spent the morning with us, and most of afternoon. Auntie Audrey also came up and stayed for dinner. Mum sewed all day again today, and fixed up two dresses for me. Audrey and I read a lot of "Kenilworth". It is getting very interesting. Dad was away in Goodna nearly all day.

Wednesday 15

Audrey and I read all the morning. Just about dinnertime, Morgan arrived to stay for a few days. Auntie Audrey went to Brisbane again and saw Pte J. Cooms. It was rainified all day, and in afternoon, there was a big wind storm, also 25 points of rain. The wind did a good deal of harm. Blew millions of mangoes off, ruined a lot of Bris. Botanical Gardens, and a soldier was killed at Chermside Camp. Audrey and I went up to Campbells at night. Audrey and I cooked (failures).

Thursday 16

Rained nearly all day, in fits and starts, but good, substantial showers - about 194 points here altogether. Mum and Audrey drove to town and got drenched coming home. Morgan and I went up to Campbells for the day. We helped make the Xmas Cake. Made some cocoanut ice this morning. Got some nice Xmas cards to send away, and Audrey got an autograph.

Friday 17

Morgan went back to Goodna this morning with Dad. Barnsies (2 girls) came down and spent the day with us. A few light showers fell. Mum and I washed (a whopper) all day, and I did a bit of housework this morning. Got a letter from Thelma T., a Xmas Card from Edna Hadley, and my report (a really nice one). Audrey went to Goodna in morning.

Saturday 18

Mum and I ironed nearly all day. Mum's back was very bad again. Audrey went up to Farm with Keith and Jim and came home at night with Aunties Audrey and Ivy, who stayed for a while. Got some more mail today. Days passing pretty quickly lately. Goodnight.

Sunday 19

Mum stayed in bed nearly all day. In afternoon, Meyrick (in uniform), Zilpha H., Aunties Audrey and Ivy were over and played tennis.

Monday 20

Did a good deal of packing and mending. Audrey and I finished "Kenilworth" tonight. It was just lovely but Amy Robsart shouldn't have been killed. Audrey and I cleaned all the silver in the afternoon. I marked a lot of clothes for Manly. Got some mail again this morning. Won't be long now until we get to Manly. Mum's back better than before.

Tuesday 21
Worked hard all day. We did the washing and ironing, cooked, made chutney, Xmas Pudding etc.. Audrey and I walked over to Presentation Meeting at school with Auntie Audrey and Ivy, but hardly any one turned up, so was postponed. Lovely moonlight night. Got some mail.

Wednesday 22
Did all the packing today for Manly tomorrow. Ma and Keith came down and stayed for dinner. Did a bit of washing and ironing. Tom up nearly all day. Dad went to town in afternoon, and didn't get home til late. Got some mail again today. Audrey and Merv went up to Farm at night, and Aunties Audrey and Ivy came home with them. Had a whole roast fowl for tea.

Thursday 23
Came to Goodna in cart. Met Auntie Rosie on Goodna station, on arrival from Einasleigh and had a bit of talk to her before our train arrived. Then came (8.18 train) to Manly (11.30), where we took cab to "Retreat". Had a bathe on arrival and devoured chuckey. I had a headache, so we slept for 1½ hours in afternoon, then Audrey and I went shopping. At night we all went for walk to jetty (bonser new one).

Friday 24
Got up late. Had breakfast, and after a while went in for a bathe. It was a gl-or-i-ous one this time. No jelly-fish at all so far. Had awfully late dinner (bacon and eggs). Rested all afternoon and read. We all went on Pier at night, then on to the Pictures, where we met Mr and Mrs Ingram. Then went onto Pier again.

Saturday 25
Had breakfast and after a while went in for a bathe as yesterday. We stayed in for ages. Then we took dinner with us to other side of Manly and had it there. Read there and talked until after 4. Elwyn Parry was with us, and we met the rest of them (the Parrys). Went onto Pier at night, where there was some music, etc.

Sunday 26

Had another bonser bathe this morning and knitted on beach. Then after dinner did the same, only Elwyn was talking to us. Went onto jetty at night, where had fun listening to soldier boys.

Monday 27

Boxing day, and there were crowds of people down. Merv and I went to meet 10.30 train, and coming back met a soldier and civilian who knew us, but whom we didn't know. Went for several walks and brought Mrs Parry and 2 chil. home to dinner. In afternoon, 3 Hilliers and Miss Phillips were up to see us, and they and I went to dance in Picture Hall and then onto Pier. Had great fun with Zilpha and Elwyn. Merv and I went to Pictures at night, but had to stand all the time. Rained a bit at night. Big boat races today, and "Torment" won the Cup. (I got a great pile of mail).

Tuesday 28

Audrey and I went up to meet 10.30 train, which Meyrick was supposed to come down on. But he never turned up, so we met 12.30 train, but all in vain. He didn't come at all. After dinner went in for a bathe, but was so shallow we came almost straight out again. In afternoon, Audrey and I knitted and read on beach. It was lovely. Much quieter than it has been. We all went to Pictures at night. They were pretty good, and we got a good seat. Met Elwyn and Bob Knight both coming and going (caught them nicely).

Wednesday 29

Got up very late and had breakfast. Audrey and I had several trips down town, and once met Hywel (Parry), who took us up to camp to see Ceridwen. Bought some nice cherries. I wrote and posted a lot of letters. Wrote and read and knitted on beach. It was lovely. Then we all went early to Wynnum. Merv went to the Pictures there and we put in time waiting for him by viewing side-shows, etc,. and listening to music on Pier. First time we've been to Wynnum since been down.

Thursday 30

Audrey and I went out shopping in morning. Isabel McDonnell and Mrs Frost were at "Retreat" when we left. Mum washed and had a general clean up. Aud. and I went up to Post Office in afternoon, and we met Elwyn who told us Mat. Kerwin was down. We then read on Pier until nearly seven o'clock. Went onto Pier at night, where we met Mat. I had a bit of a malty with Elwyn. Audrey had a play on piano.

Friday 31

Got up very late. After breakfast, Audrey and I went out shopping, and met Hywel, to whom we gave some magazines and fruit. Then we read for ever so long, and then in for a bathe. Mum went out shopping about 4 o'clock. After tea, we went to the Pictures, which were very good, especially "The Conquest of Quebec". Then went onto the Pier, where Audrey (aged 13) played the New Year in and Sgt Coyle gave her a lovely box of chocolates.

Saturday 1

Got up early and had a bathe. Merv and I went up to station in morning, but didn't see many we knew. Had a talk to Gunner Betland. Rested until after 3, when we went onto jetty. Merv went over to King Island on one boat and I went over with Elwyn on next. I brought him back to tea, and we all went onto jetty at night, where the Bris. Concert Band was playing.

Sunday 2

Got up early again and had a bathe. Audrey and I sat on beach in morning, and made up poetry and wrote a letter to Ivy. We all rested all the afternoon, and then went onto the jetty at night, where we again met Elwyn.

This was the start of a lifetime habit for Queenie - keeping a diary.

Endnotes

1. McGarvie, Graham (ed) McGarvie Family History 1844-1994. Graham McGarvie, 1995

2. Kennedy, Thalia. *The First One Hundred Years.* Brisbane; Boolarong Publications 1991.

3. Morrison, W. Frederic. *Aldine History of Queensland.* Vol. II 1888. p.424.

4. Ipswich City Council. *Expanded Ipswich Heritage Study (CD Rom)* 1998. p. 1042.

5. McGarvie, p. 53.

6. Much of the family information has been provided by Claire Wilson (Queenie's daughter) and Valma Jackson (Queenie's sister).

7. Roll book of Ipswich Girls' Grammar School.

8. Kennedy, pp. 103-4.

9. Kennedy, p. 19.

10. Kennedy, p. 24.

11. Kennedy, p. 24.

12. Buchanan, Robyn. *Ipswich Remembers.* Ipswich City Council and the Australia Remembers Committee, 1995. p. 6.